THE GOLDEN LOTUS

AND

OTHER LEGENDS OF JAPAN

BY

EDWARD GREEY

AUTHOR OF "YOUNG AMERICANS IN JAPAN," "THE WONDERFUL CITY OF TOKIO," ETC., AND ONE OF THE TRANSLATORS OF THE JAPANESE HISTORICAL ROMANCE "THE LOYAL RONINS"

Cover Designed and Drawn by the Author

**Fredonia Books
Amsterdam, The Netherlands**

The Golden Lotus and Other Legends of Japan

by
Edward Greey

ISBN: 1-4101-0130-4

Copyright © 2003 by Fredonia Books

Reprinted from the 1883 edition

Fredonia Books
Amsterdam, The Netherlands
http://www.fredoniabooks.com

All rights reserved, including the right to reproduce this book, or portions thereof, in any form.

In order to make original editions of historical works available to scholars at an economical price, this facsimile of the original edition of 1883 is reproduced from the best available copy and has been digitally enhanced to improve legibility, but the text remains unaltered to retain historical authenticity.

PREFACE.

THE Japanese say, "The *bozu* [priest] and the *hanashika* [professional story-teller] can pick a man's pocket with their tongues"; *i. e.*, the stories told by those men are so amusing and admirable that the people empty their purses in order to reward the priest for his sermons and the vagabond for his recitations.

In this book I have endeavored to reproduce some of the "Legends of the Land of the Rising Sun," as related by the *bozu* and *hanashika*. In addition, I have assumed the rôle of *saimon*, and described scenes in the life of the modern Japanese.

EDWARD GREEY.

20 East Seventeenth Street, New York.

CONTENTS.

	PAGES
LEGEND OF THE GOLDEN LOTUS	7–15
THE TOAD OF TOMIOKA	16–27
THE HANASHIKA (*Professional Story-Teller*) . . .	28–41
LEGEND OF LU-WEN, THE WOOD-CUTTER	42–53
A JAPANESE DELICACY	54–66
A LEGEND OF THE RAIN	67–81
STREET SCENES IN TOKIO	82–94
A VISIT TO A JAPANESE THEATRE	95–104
LEGENDS OF THE GOD-FOX	105–115
NO GAKU (*Ancient Opera of Japan*)	116–131
SHINDA USAGI-UMA (*Legend of the Dead Ass*) . . .	132–145

LEGEND OF THE GOLDEN LOTUS.

HEAVY drops of rain were plashing upon the dusty surface of the broad avenue of Shiba, Tokio. The pilgrims, who but a few moments before thronged the place, had vanished like "water in sand" into the adjoining restaurants; and the sellers of nondescript trifles, located beneath the magnificent trees, were anxiously glancing skyward, and hurriedly covering their wares with sheets of oiled paper.

My companion, a charming old Japanese gentleman, knitted his bushy eyebrows, bowed, smiled, and said in a gentle tone, "A hundred thousand pardons! I believe we are about to have a down-pour. I regret very much this inhospitable weather. Would you like to partake of a cup of tea?"

While he was speaking the rain began to descend in a torrent; whereupon we sought refuge in the nearest *chaya*, which was crowded with men and women in white robes.

We seated ourselves in a retired corner, and as we sipped our tea, listened to the babel of conversation around us. Presently a young *bozu* (priest) entered, and after shaking the moisture from his robes, said, —

"It is almost time for the *ho-dan* (sermon); you, good people, ought not to miss such a great benefit."

He was a plump, mild-featured lad, and his head was so closely shaven that it almost pained one to look at it.

The pilgrims, who, upon his entrance, had bowed their foreheads to the mats, murmured respectful replies, and rising, awaited his departure.

To my surprise he turned to my companion, and said, "All men ought to know of Buddha. It would be a benevolent act for you to induce that foreign gentleman to listen to the golden words. Who knows but that he might be led into the true path?"

My friend, who blushed to the tips of his ears, made a respectful gesture of caution, and whispered behind his fan, "Reverend sir, this gentleman understands what you say."

The *bozu*, not at all disconcerted, bowed politely and invited me to accompany him, remarking, "We have many of your preachers in our country: surely you will not object to listen to one of ours."

I replied that I had long wished to have such an opportunity, and that I should be most happy to accept his invitation.

While we were waiting for the shower to pass over,

we had quite an interesting conversation; and when I hinted that his class had neglected to teach the masses the pure doctrines of Buddhism, and had allowed the people to remain in a shocking state of idolatry, he said, "I think you have been misinformed, or do not quite understand the movement that is taking place in our religious circles. It is true, before the arrival of you foreign gentlemen, there was great laxity among some of our sects; now all of us are doing our best to instruct our people in the Great Truth": adding, "The rain has ceased, honorable sir from afar: will you please accompany me and listen to the imperfect teaching of a humble follower of Shaka?"

It was a novel sensation to find myself one of a procession of pilgrims, while the conversation of our devout companions severely taxed my gravity.

"*Hai* [yes]," said a weather-beaten dame, "those dark-eyed *to-jin* [foreigners] are always more amenable to reason than the *oni* [imps] with blue eyes. In fact, they are more human" (utterly disregarding the cautioning signals of my friend). "I am one of those who speak my mind. Nobody frightens me by scowling."

"Pray excuse her," whispered the worthy old gentleman. "Some people are so religious that they have enough faith for half a dozen. Such persons have very little sense"; adding *sotto voce*, "but then, she is only a woman."

After a short walk we reached a shed-like building connected with one of the temples. Our guide ushered us in and saw us seated comfortably on the clean matted floor, then retired behind a screen at the upper end of the apartment.

The pilgrims behaved very much like our country folks at a church meeting. Some prayed, others stared about them, and a few yawned as though they considered the affair a bore.

After a brief interval an ascetic-visaged *bozu* glided from behind the screen, and advancing to a platform slightly raised above the level of the floor, knelt, bowed, and murmured the Buddhist prayer; then sitting up on his heels, glanced round at the congregation until he discovered me. This action reminded me of an incident I had once witnessed in a place of worship in far-off Massachusetts, and I smiled.

The *bozu* regarded me sorrowfully, after which he began his discourse in a low, musical voice, saying, —

"Man is born without a knowledge of Amida [Buddha], therefore it is the teacher's duty to instruct everybody, not only in the true doctrine, but also to enlighten people concerning the life of the Lord Shaka-ni-yorai.

"I will not insult your intelligence by telling you who Shaka was. Every child knows that" (glancing slyly at me). "The wonderful story of his life has been translated into all the languages of the world. Everybody knows how the king gave up his title and became a beggar, that he might give the true light to the world.

"Of late years we have had strange teachers coming from various foreign countries, offering us their religion" (slyly) "and their merchandise. What can they give you more precious and delightful than the Golden Lotus?" (In a chatty tone.)

"A few days ago I met a pilgrim who said to me, 'Holy Father, tell me about the Golden Lotus. I do not understand why the Lord Shaka is seated upon that beautiful flower.'

"This ignorance amazed me; however, after I had told him the truth, I thought, 'Possibly there may be many in our land as ignorant as he,' therefore I made up my mind, the next time I spoke to the people, to explain this portion of the life of Shaka-ni-yorai." (Very solemnly, with half-closed eyes.)

"The merciful Lord Shaka had concluded his meditations on the mountain of Dan-doku, and was descending the rocky path on his way toward the city. Night was approaching, the shadows were deepening, and no sound disturbed the stillness of the hour.

"As he reached a plateau at the crest of the last turn in the road, he heard some one exclaim in a loud voice, '*Shio-giyo mu-jiyo!* [The outward manner is not always an index to the natural disposition.]'

"The Lord Shaka was amazed and delighted, thinking, 'What manner of being is this? I must question him and learn more.'

"He then approached the edge of the precipice, still hearing the voice repeating the wonderful sentence. On glancing down into the valley he beheld a horrible *tatsu* [dragon], which regarded him threateningly."

The *bozu* changed his tone into a confidential one, and glancing at me, said,—

"I will now explain the meaning of the dragon's words.

"Man is naturally disposed to sin, and if he were left without teaching would descend to the lowest depths of degradation. The Lord Shaka came into the world to teach humility, gentleness, forbearance, and patience. Those who listen to his words will gradually lose their natural disposition to sin and approach one step nearer to the Golden Lotus. This is the true explanation of '*Shio-giyo mu-jiyo.*'"

(Resuming his solemn manner.) "'The Lord Shaka seated himself upon the edge of the rock, and addressing the monster, said, 'How came you to learn one of the higher mysteries of Buddhism? Although I have been studying ten years, I have never heard this sentence. I think you must know others. Please tell them to me.'

"The dragon coiled itself tightly round the base of the rock, then said in a thunderous tone, '*Ze-shio metsu-po!* [All living things are antagonistic to the law of Buddha.]'"

(Resuming his confidential manner.) "This truth is eternal. How sad it is to know that every year millions of people die ignorant of the teachings of the Lord Shaka! I beseech you to keep the laws of Buddha, and to close your ears to the words of false priests who come from outside the civilized world to encourage the worst inclination of human nature, — that is, the violation of the Buddhistic law."

This covert allusion to our missionaries was much relished by the old woman who had spoken her mind so freely. "*Hai* [yes]," she exclaimed, glancing fixedly at me, "yes, yes, yes, that is so!"

The preacher again resumed his earnest manner, saying: —

"'*Ze-shio metsu-po!*' roared the dragon, regarding the sacred one. Then it held its peace for a space, whereupon the Lord Shaka said, 'That is very good; now pray tell me the next sentence.'

"'*Shio-metsu metsu-i!* [All living things must die.]'

"The Lord Shaka bowed and answered, 'That sentence is better than the last; I would very much like to hear the next.'

"The dragon looked up at him with a hungry expression, and said, 'The next truth is the last and most precious, but I cannot speak it until my hunger is appeased. I have not eaten since daybreak, and am very weak. Give me some food and I will tell you the last of the four precious sentences.'

"'I will give you anything you wish,' replied the Lord Shaka. 'You have such great wisdom that I will deny you nothing. What do you demand?'

"'Human flesh,' was the response.

"The Lord Shaka regarded the dragon pityingly, and said, 'My religion forbids me to destroy life; but as I must, for the sake of the people, hear the final sentence, I will give myself to you. Now tell me all you know.'

"The monster opened its enormous mouth, and as it did so, said, '*Jaku-metsu I-raku!* [The greatest happiness is experienced after the soul has left the body.]'

"The Lord Shaka listened, then bowed his sacred head and sprang into the gaping mouth of the *tatsu*.

"When he touched the dragon's jaws they split into eight parts, and changed into the eight petals of the Golden Lotus."

(Earnestly and solemnly.) "As the Lord Shaka trusted himself to the horrible monster, so you must trust to His teachings. If you do so, and earnestly strive to attain perfection, you will, most assuredly, some day, learn the full meaning of the sentence, '*Jakumetsu I-raku!*'"

A collection was made for the benefit of the preacher, after which the congregation silently dispersed.

When we reached the avenue, my companion remarked, "Although I am only an ignorant man, I cannot help making comparisons. After all, there is not much difference between our religions. You hope for a crown of glory, and I to some day take my place upon a Golden Lotus."

THE TOAD OF TOMIOKA.

ABOUT seven miles from Yokohama, down the picturesque bay of Yedo, is the famous holiday resort of Tomioka, much frequented by overworked merchants fleeing from the brain-wearying excitement of the tea business, *blasé* globe-trotters, and ruddy-faced sea-captains anxious to learn something of the inner life of the Japanese; for in that delightfully retired spot, *chaya* (tea houses) are plentiful, the attendants are obliging, and the air is surcharged with ozone and asceticism. The visitor sleeps in a temple, bathes in the blue waters of the bay, and when he takes his meals listens alternately to the pretty conceits of his cherry-lipped servitor and to the soothing drone of the *bozu* (priests) repeating their monotonous prayer, "*Namu Amida Butsu!*" (Hail, Omnipotent Buddha!)

One spring morning I was lying prone upon the soft mats of a rear apartment in the temple of Cho-sho, enjoying the delightful sensations resulting from a plunge in the surf and the contemplation of one of those wonderful examples of Japanese patience, a "miniature garden." Before me, in a space about six feet by four, was a charming landscape containing hills, dales, and a mountain stream and lake; the former dotted with tiny clumps of feathery bamboo, artistically interspersed with gnarled, twisted, dwarfed *matsu* (pine-trees), and the latter spanned by a stone bridge, the approach to which was ornamented with two diminutive granite *toro* (lanterns). In the distance, standing out in bold relief against the blue sky, was a model of "glorious Fuji-yama," whose white peak towered so naturally above the greenery that I almost imagined I was looking at the mountain itself.

As I gazed upon the pretty scene, I noticed something move at the base of a beetling cliff on the left, and presently beheld an enormous toad, which, slowly emerging from its cool retreat, came hopping down a winding path that had evidently been made for its special accommodation.

It was a solemn-looking creature, with a rich brown and yellow skin and a body as plump as the *bozu*, my landlord, who took such minute pains with the flowerless paradise in which the *kawadzu* resided.

Although the Japanese devote much time and labor to producing arboreous monstrosities, they seldom attempt to reduce the size of "nature's gems," or to introduce them among their mimic landscapes, deeming blossoms to be out of place amid such surroundings.

The toad hopped a short distance toward me, then, halting abruptly, "corrected its attitude," as the Japanese term it, — *i. e.*, sat up in a respectful position, — and eyed me askance, evidently comprehending that I was a *to-jin* (foreigner). At first it gaped slightly, as though amazed; after which it recovered its usual placidity, and slowly winked one eye as much as to say, "This is my hour for feeding, and I do not intend to postpone my enjoyment for any one."

Once more advancing, it came flop, flop, flop down the winding path, and on landing upon the little bridge sat up as before, closed its eyes, and appeared to listen to the droning prayer of the *bozu*.

While I was watching the creature, O Fuji-nami (Miss Waves-of-the-wistaria-blossom), one of the waitresses of the *chaya* from which I procured my meals, noiselessly entered the apartment, knelt beside me, placed a tray upon the floor, and bowing her head to the mats, murmured, "Honorable Mister from afar, your breakfast is served."

O Fuji-nami was a gentle-mannered, sweet-tempered girl of sixteen, with large brown eyes, and a well-shaped oval face which, according to custom, was liberally covered with bismuth, while on the centre of her pouting lower lip was a dab of carmine that contrasted painfully with the dazzling whiteness of her complexion. She was dressed quite gayly in silk and crêpe *kimono* (garments), and brilliant *obi* (girdle), and was a charming specimen of her class.

Upon hearing her voice I half rose, turned my face toward her, leaned my cheek upon my hand, and bidding her good morning, inquired if she had ever seen the toad.

Instead of replying immediately, she sat up on her heels, sighed, glanced downward until her long eyelashes veiled her beautiful eyes, and thus remained, as though thinking over some very painful incident; then, after a pause, said in a gentle, sad voice, "Yes, I know the unfortunate O Momo [Miss Peach]. Alas! that one so lovely should be compelled to assume such a garb and" (shuddering) "to cat flies."

This speech aroused my curiosity, and I begged her to explain herself; when she whispered, as though afraid the toad would overhear her, —

"Three years ago a foreign *sama* [gentleman], with hair like the sunset in August, came to stay here. He was very kind, and we all liked him because he addressed us by our proper names, and never called us 'Way-tare' or 'Kome-ear.' My friend, O Momo, was a very beautiful girl, and was quite romantic. One day I discovered her weeping, and upon inquiring the cause, learned that she was in love with our golden-haired visitor. Oh! Charlie Smith *Sama* was very handsome. Perhaps you know him."

I explained that Smith was not an uncommon name in the States; whereupon she sighed, shook her head sadly, and continued, —

"He remained here long after the other *to-jin* [foreigners] had departed."

Then she paused, covered her face with the ample sleeves of her *kimono*, and wept softly.

The term *to-jin* (literally "a Chinaman") is not considered a respectful one, and is seldom used by the Japanese when speaking to a foreigner. It is, however, so commonly employed by them in their ordinary conversation, that they in familiar talk with us often employ the word without thinking of its contemptuous meaning. It is sometimes applied to objectionable things, such as new diseases, strange insects, etc.

After O Fuji-nami had recovered from her emotion, she continued, —

"Only the gods know what causes women to love as they do. Poor O Momo! When Smith *Sama* left us, he vowed to return the following summer; but though she was always on the watch when the boats from Yokohama landed their passengers on the beach below, the golden-haired stranger came not, and her heart sank. She, who had always been merry, grew sad and lost her beauty. The unhappy one waited until the leaves of the maples changed to the color of Charlie Smith *Sama's* hair; then one night, when the moon was smiling on the water of the bay, she filled her sleeves with stones and sought peace beneath the silvery waves. Two days afterward her body returned to us for burial. We girls subscribed for a *saké* tub [commonly used as a coffin among the lower orders of Japanese], and the good *bozu* performed the services for half their usual fees. Alas that her spirit should now inhabit the body of that toad!"

"How?" I inquired.

"Yes!" (in a very low tone, glancing at the reptile, which still appeared to be listening to us,) "you may think it strange, but yonder *kawadzu* is poor O Momo. On the day of her burial she appeared in that place, and she has never left the spot" (very sadly). "She is waiting for Charlie Smith *Sama* to return. I believe he was a wizard."

Her grief was too genuine and her manner too earnest to provoke a smile; so I comforted her by saying I would take every care of the toad, and endeavor to discover the destroyer of poor O Momo's peace of mind. As I was speaking my attention was attracted by the reptile, which was sitting motionless on the bridge with its mouth slightly open, "yanking" in the flies that were dancing merrily in the sunbeams overhead. It looked so serene and self-satisfied that I could not believe it had ever liked any object more romantic than a fat blue-bottle.

"Is she not beautiful?" murmured O Fuji-nami. "How hard she must have found it to acquire a taste for such food!"

Just then a big miller fluttered on to the scene and settled upon one of the dwarf *matsu* (pines). Presto! a long, thin, red tongue darted from between the parted jaws of the toad, and in a second the moth was transferred to the cavernous mouth.

It required more faith than I had to imagine that the spirit animating the fat, overgorged *kawadzu* had ever inhabited the pretty "soul-case" of O Momo, though O Fuji-nami evidently believed such to be a fact.

It was a comical scene: the reptile mechanically blinking at us, with the wings of the miller protruding from its mouth and a smug expression on its features; the girl, with big tears coursing down her bismuth-coated face, sadly regarding the ugly brute; and myself sympathizing with her and pretending to believe her story.

While I ate my breakfast she related some wonderful tales concerning the *kawadzu*, which she assured me was gifted with almost supernatural wisdom.

"O Momo can foretell an earthquake or a storm, can indicate how long you have to live and whether you will be lucky or unlucky in your affairs."

"Indeed!"

"Oh, yes, *Sama!* she is the dearest, wisest, most gentle being in the world, and is known far and near as the Toad of Tomioka."

When I finished my frugal meal, O Fuji-nami knelt, bowed her head to the mats, returned the bowls to the tray, and rising, retired with her burden, leaving me to think about her story and to watch the reptile.

Away down on the beach I could hear the laughter of the bathers, and nearer, in the main hall of the temple, the dull hum of the *bozu* at their prayers; while in the little garden all was still save the beforementioned flies, and they were one by one rapidly disappearing down the capacious throat of the motionless *kawadzu*.

As I was lazily contemplating the creature, a small shadow flashed across the landscape, and something alighted among the greenery and vanished behind the feathery bamboos, from whence presently proceeded a low "buzz," evidently music to the ears of the gentle O Momo.

It turned, sat up, looked at me over the back of its head, and rolled its goggle eyes as though saying,

"Listen, my friend from afar. That is the song of a blue-bottle."

"Buzz-wuzz-wum!"

The new-comer hummed among the landscape, but did not reveal itself; finding which, the toad once more turned politely toward me, closed its mouth and eyes, and appeared to be slumbering.

"Buzz-wuzz-wuzz!" went the unseen insect.

There was something very soothing in the hum of the new arrival, and I presently became affected by it; then, all of a sudden, I awoke with a start, and beheld O Momo capture a large insect, the action being so rapidly executed that I had no opportunity of ascertaining the species of its victim. All I saw was the toad with its cheeks distended, winking knowingly and panting with excitement.

In another instant a change came over the countenance of the *kawadzu:* its eyes protruded, the corners of its mouth assumed a downward curve, and it slowly opened its jaws until it looked like a hungry squab gaping for a worm.

As it did so, O Fuji-nami entered with towels and a brass bowl containing warm water. On seeing the gestures of the toad, she quickly deposited the articles on the floor, knelt by the window-sill, clasped her hands palm to palm, and tearfully exclaimed, —

"Ye gods! she is dying!"

The *kawadzu* shook its head, tried to insert its hind toes in its mouth, turned over on its back, sat up against one of the lanterns like a puppy learning to beg, and made a wheezing noise; then, happy thought! endeavored to dislodge its victim by spitting. I have witnessed some very lame attempts, but never more impotent ones than those made by that toad, which, spite of the popular belief, "could n't spit worth a cent." Meanwhile the imprisoned insect was working away like a woodpecker.

"Oh, what shall I do?" moaned the waitress. "Poor, poor O Momo! She will be killed, and perhaps have to be a snake in her next state."

While she was sobbing and lamenting, one of the *bozu*, an ascetic-faced old fellow, looked in at the door and inquired the cause of her agony. On ascertaining the trouble he entered the room, knelt, bowed his head to the mats, and sitting upon his heels, said, —

"Probably the amiable creature is bewitched."

Knowing this was meant for me, and not being desirous of earning fame as a wizard, I asked him to examine the reptile. He took a pair of *hashi* (chopsticks) from a shelf, advanced to the edge of the mats, reached forward, dexterously grasped the toad with the instruments, raised it from the ground, and peered into its gaping mouth. Turning his shaven head toward me, he smiled until his face resembled an animated cobweb and I could scarcely see his twinkling eyes; then once more bowing, said,—

"See how weak women are. When this miserable creature was in the more perfect state, she became enamored of a red-headed *to-jin;* now" (chuckling) "she has mistaken a *to-jin hai*" (foreign fly) "for a blue-bottle. *Namu Amida Butsu!*"

He placed the toad upon its back on the mats, inserted the *hashi* in its mouth, and released the cause of its emotion,— a big, vigorous yellow-jacket. These pests are said to have been introduced into Japan by foreigners, hence their name.

The wasp lay for a moment all of a heap, with its wings adhering to its slender limbs and striped body; after which it stretched itself, vibrated its flying apparatus, and crawling to the window-sill, buzzed derisively, soared across the little landscape, and vanished over the peak of Fuji into the blue distance.

The *bozu* directed O Fuji-nami to bathe the toad in the warm water; having done which he retired to his cell, murmuring as he went, "*Namu Amida Butsu!*"

Upon looking at the girl I saw she was weeping, and on my inquiring the cause, she said,—

"I wish I were a man! Everything is against us

women. I believe that *to-jin hai* was Charlie Smith *Sama!* Not contented with causing poor O Momo's death in her former life, he has returned to torment her in this. Alas! alas! men know not how to love!"

After a while the *kawadzu* sat up and eyed me reproachfully, as though I were the cause of its swollen head; then it slowly hopped up the pathway and disappeared into its retreat beneath the rocks.

That was the last I saw of the Toad of Tomioka.

THE HANASHIKA.

(PROFESSIONAL STORY-TELLER.)

THE sun was beating fiercely upon the heavily tiled roof of the temple of Sen-so, the ever-merciful Kuwannon, in Asakusa, one of the most celebrated places in the ancient city of Tokio. From amid the cool recesses of the carved and gilded beams of the porch came the soft cooing of the opal-breasted doves, which were dreamily enjoying the delights of their shady retreat; and from the interior of the dimly lighted structure issued thin blue clouds of incense, and a gentle murmur like the drone of bees hovering over flowers, — the voices of the *bozu* (priests) at their devotions.

No other sounds disturbed the holy calm of the place, and no pilgrims were to be seen on the broad flagged pathway leading to the main edifice. The girls who sold beans and rice for the sacred birds and animals were dozing by their stands; the dealers in rosaries, dolls, prayer-books, novels, sacred pictures, photographs of the Mikado and of celebrated actors, incense, and bay rum, were slumbering with one eye open, in order to enjoy a brief repose and at the same time watch the thieves who infest the spot. The withered crones, who had all the morning been howling prayers to attract the attention of the charitable, were resting from their labors and employing their toothless gums in the mastication of their frugal meal of cold boiled rice.

I had spent several hours in the temple, had my fortune told by the priests, inspected the well-polished image of Bindzuri (one of the *Jin-roku Rakan*, sixteen disciples of Buddha reputed to have the power of curing all disease), and gazed on the shrine said to contain the little image of Kuwannon that, twelve centuries ago, was fished out of the Asakusa River by Hashi-no Nakatomo, who founded the original edifice.

Truth to tell, I was tired of the Buddhist show and anxious to listen to something more exciting than the monotonous prayer of the priests; so, quitting the neighborhood of the temple, I wandered into the shady grounds and presently found myself before an open booth, on the floor of which squatted a group of people listening to the recital of a professional story-teller.

Notwithstanding the counter attractions of the modern stage, cheap sensational literature, and the introduction of daily newspapers, the *hanashika* holds his own in the affections of the masses, and is as popular as he was a thousand years ago; for while relating one of the tales of old Japan, the story-teller can covertly criticise passing events and express sentiments that find a warm response in the hearts of his hearers.

When the man had ended his narrative, I slipped off my shoes and joined his patrons; noticing which, he bowed respectfully and bade his attendant serve me with tea.

He was seated on a low rostrum at the back of the booth, which was made of split bamboo mats laid on a framework of light poles, and was admirably arranged to exclude the sun and admit the air. Before him stood a *tsukuye* (table) about six inches high, upon which he rapped, drummed, or rattled to emphasize the more thrilling portions of his recitals; and on his right was a lower platform occupied by his attendant, who replenished the charcoal in the *hibachi* (fire bowl), supplied his master with tea, and handed around the fan for contributions.

The audience was composed of pilgrims, merchants out for a day's enjoyment, and boys of various ages. All were grave in their demeanor, polite to one another, and inveterate smokers.

After a considerable sum in brass *tempo* (oval coins worth less than a cent) and cash (*cho-moku*) had been collected by the attendant, the *hanashika* bowed until his forehead touched the low table, then said, —

"Honorable sirs, you doubtless imagine you are about to receive great pleasure for your trifling outlay of money, and expect that I will alternately cause you to gape with amazement, shudder with terror, and laugh until you exhibit the roots of your tongues. Yes, yes, I mean to give you the full value of your money. My stories are *jetsu-roku* [true history], not like *zu-zan* [so called from Zu, a notorious Chinese who forged historical records]; my art, like the silken cord of the rosary, connects facts and makes them a harmonious whole, illustrating the virtues of fidelity, patriotism, and valor. Now listen attentively, and endeavor to understand the full meaning of my narrative."

He closed his fan, once more saluted gravely, then began in a musical voice, "The night guard over the gates of the sacred city of Kioto had grown negligent, and the *oni* [demons] frequently entered the precincts and carried off persons who were unfortunately compelled to be abroad after sunset" (In a significant aside.) "We no longer have any necessity for guards over our city gates: the latter have been removed, and the *oni* can enter and depart at all hours. *Hai!* [yes] this is truly a period of change. However, let us be thankful for all things sent by the gods."

This covert hit at foreigners caused his audience to murmur approvingly and to throw him a shower of coins. The lower orders of Japanese do not love us, and though exceedingly polite, delight in slyly expressing their feelings. Having put his patrons in a good-humor, and shown that while tolerating my presence, his heart was filled with *Yamato damashi* (the spirit of Japan), he rapped the table with his fan, and bowing, recommenced, plunging boldly into his story : —

"The night was cool and the sky was clouded when Watanabe Tsuna, one of the faithful soldiers of Raiko, chief captain of the imperial guard, started for the Rajo gate at the southwestern entrance to the palace of Kioto. The wind demons skulked amid the branches of the pines, and shrieked menacingly as the brave soldier strode along the deserted path which was overshadowed by the massive battlements; but Watanabe knew no fear, for he carried at his side a wonderful sword forged by the great Yukihira.

"Upon reaching his post he examined his weapons, and taking an amulet from his sleeve, wound it about the hilt of his *katana* [long sword], then exclaimed defiantly, 'Hundred million demons advance!' The *oni* heard this and trembled; for his face was illuminated with the glow of courage, and they also feared the power of the sacred charm. The demons consulted, like old women who had heard bad news, and gnashed their teeth. They had sworn to enter the city that night and carry off a beautiful virgin who was coveted by the hideous, red-haired-monster, Shu-ten-doji, their master.

"'Wait, wait, wait,' murmured one of their number, an old *oni* with only one eye and teeth like a dragon's claws. 'If we keep quiet, Watanabe will soon fall asleep; then we can attack and kill him, and accomplish our task.'

"The others thought this advice was good, and held their breath; so Watanabe heard nothing but the amorous chirping of the night cricket and the love song of the frogs 'cloaping' in the moat below. 'Ah!' he thought, 'if I only had my tablets in my sleeve, I would write a poem.

"'High in the *matsu* [pine] chirps — what?
Low in the moat sings — what?
The eager lover.'

"Watanabe, like many great warriors, was a poet; and as composing verses absorbs the soul, he was presently lost in deep thought and soon slumbered. At that moment the one-eyed *oni* crept to the gate, reached its long, hairy arm round the door-post, grasped Watanabe by the helmet, and —"

Here the *hanashika* paused, and bowing respectfully, murmured, "Five *tempo*, honorable sirs, and I will continue the story. For the mean and trifling sum of five *tempo* you shall learn what the *oni* did to Watanabe."

He closed his fan, signalled to his attendant to hand him a cup of tea, and leaning his elbows upon the table, watched the faces of his audience. The pilgrims fumbled in their pouches and sent their coins spinning on the mat before him, shouted " *Yuke* " (go on), and looked as eager as a lot of school-boys listening to a ghost story. After the last coin had fallen, he squirted the tea from his mouth and continued in a low, " creepy " voice, —

"The *oni* endeavored to raise Watanabe from the ground. Meanwhile the clouds had gathered around them, the demons were hurrying to their comrade's aid, and the sky was filled with their exultant cries." (Rattling his fan on the *tsukuye*.) " The undaunted soldier raised his left hand and grasped the *oni's* wrist, then quickly drawing his sword, made a cut that whistled like the autumn wind among the trees, and severed his assailant's arm. The monster, howling with pain, sprang upon a cloud, and with its companions vanished, leaving Watanabe regarding his bloody trophy. When morning dawned he returned to the castle, and laying the arm at Raiko's feet, murmured, ' Accept this as a proof of my watchfulness.'

" Raiko commended him highly, and observed, ' It is

said if you keep an *oni's* limb apart from its stump for a week, it will no longer have power to reunite itself to the creature's body. Guard that carefully; for as long as you possess it, the demons will be unable to enter our holy city.'

"Watanabe bowed, conveyed his prize home and placed it in a stone chest, which he securely bound with a rope of rice straw procured from a neighboring temple. He watched his treasure day and night, and grew red-eyed with his vigil. On the third evening he heard a faint noise outside his house, and the voice of his old *oba* [aunt], exclaiming, 'Let me in, Tsuna! I wish to see the arm of the *oni*, and to compliment you upon your prowess.'

"Watanabe, who greatly venerated the aged, drew aside the sliding door, and admitting her said, 'Honorable aunt, much as I would like to gratify you, I cannot exhibit my treasure until the expiration of a week.'

"'Alas!' exclaimed his visitor, who was no other than the *oni* disguised as his relative, 'I fear I shall not be able to see you then: I have come a long distance, and my limbs are very weak.'

"As she spoke, her tears fell in torrents." (Slyly, speaking satirically from the left corner of his mouth.) "Honorable masters, beware of a woman who cries too easily : she is usually an *oni* in disguise."

"*Hai* [yes]," shouted the audience.

"Watanabe again expressed his sorrow at not being able to comply with her request; on hearing which she beat her wrinkled breast and tore her scanty hair until he, moved by her grief and despair, yielded." (Speaking out of the left corner of his mouth.) "Never be deceived by a woman's tears: the man who commits such an act of folly is lost. Of course I except the honorable mother: always obey her, but" (slyly) "be firm with your wives, your sisters, cousins, and aunts, and the rest of the deceitful sex." (Lowering his voice and speaking in a mysterious tone.) "Watanabe approached the box, removed the straw rope, and partly slid aside the lid, when the crone, who had watched him with eager eyes and trembling limbs, thrust forth her left hand, and grasping the prize, shouted, 'This is my arm!'

"Uttering a derisive yell she flew out of the open door, and as she vanished into the western sky resumed her true form.

"The warrior, furious at being tricked, would have destroyed himself, but his chief persuaded him to live and to assist in killing Shu-ten-doji.

"Raiko dreamed that the possession of a celebrated sword forged by Ohara Tarudaiyu, Yasutsuna no Hoki, which had been placed in the sacred shrine of Ise by the shogun Tamura, would enable him to overcome the dreaded demon. After obtaining the weapon, he, Watanabe Tsuna, and two others disguised themselves as *komusu* [begging priests], and tracking the demon's course by the blood-marks, followed it to the pathless mountain of Oye, in Tango.

"They climbed some distance up its sides, when they came to a rivulet in which a beautiful young girl was washing the monster's garments. Raiko questioned her, and found that the *oni* devoured all the men and the old women they captured, and spared the young, whom they compelled to act as their attendants. She told the heroes how to find the cave, then resumed her occupation.

"As they warily advanced, they heard a strange, crackling noise." (Rattling his fan lightly on the table.) "Was it the rustling of the dried leaves" (hoarsely and earnestly), "or the step of a demon creeping stealthily toward them, with gleaming eyes and gaping mouth? Raiko grasped the hilt of his sword. His companions followed his example, and though their hearts beat like drums, their souls were filled with true courage and they strode forward to meet the unseen. Tramp, tramp, tramp! In another moment they turned a bend in the pathway and beheld—"

By that time the eyes of his excited audience were protruding with horror, their mouths were gaping like fishes out of water, and their fingers were clasped palm to palm; noticing which he stopped, and bowing said, "For a few *tempo* I will relate the rest of this interesting story. I have an aged mother to support, and a family of little ones."

He calmly lighted his pipe, closed his eyes, and puffed complacently, while his audience fumbled for their cash and eagerly awaited the continuation of his recital.

He was a thorough artist and a keen judge of human nature, and it was a study to watch him contemptuously elevate his pug nose when the coins were not produced fast enough.

"The best is to come," he carelessly remarked. "If my efforts are properly stimulated with plenty of *tempo*, I will alternately fill your souls with terror and cause you to shout with joy. Only ten more cash and I will resume my story."

Finally, when the spectators began to howl with indignation, he assumed a horrified expression of face and continued in a hoarse, affrighted voice, —

"Raiko and his companions trembled, for they perceived that the crackling noise came from a demon cook, who" (rattling his fan) "was breaking the bones of a human body to make soup for Shu-ten-doji.

"This sight enraged Raiko: his eyes flashed fire, his breath came quickly"; (in a loud, rapid voice) "he ascended the hill with tremendous strides, and followed by his faithful companions, soon reached the cave, the entrance to which was as ragged as the mouth of a dragon." (Quietly.) Then the hero paused and composed the following poem: —

> "'Defeats many warriors — what?
> Destroys many pleasures — what?
> Haste.'

"After doing this he became calm, and entering the cavern, beheld Shu-ten-doji seated on a pile of silken cushions, picking his huge teeth with a bone. Around him were grouped his hideous followers, while young damsels, beautiful as mermaids, were coming and going with steaming dishes of human flesh cooked in a hundred styles. Before each *oni* was a skull filled with blood, and" (hoarsely) "as these were emptied, they were refilled from tubs containing the crimson liquid.

"Raiko and his three trusty friends bowed low; then Shu-ten-doji, being too dainty a demon to eat a priest, invited them to enter and enjoy the feast.

"The visitors complied, and in order to entertain the *oni*, amused them by dancing; after which Raiko produced a bottle of drugged *saké* and politely invited their host to drink.

"When the chief demon had swallowed a skullful he passed the flask to his followers, and like them quickly yielded to its soporific effects." (In a loud voice.) "Soon their snores sounded like thunder, and the earth shook with the vibrations; hearing which" (excitedly using his fan as if it were a sword), "Raiko and his comrades threw off their disguises, and drawing their keen weapons, cut off the *oni's* heads until the floor of the cavern was waist-deep in blood, and the torrent poured over the mouth and descended into the valley" (rattling his fan in imitation of a falling stream).

"When Raiko attacked Shu-ten-doji, his sword was miraculously lengthened, his eyes flashed like spearheads in the sun, he uttered a tremendous shout, and raising the blade aloft, brought it to bear upon the hairy neck of the ghoul. As the dissevered head touched the floor of the cave, Raiko called to Watanabe to help him secure it, when to their astonishment it swelled until it became larger than the *shi-shi no kubi* [lion's head] of Kanda Miojin." (Excitedly.) "Then followed a scene that gladdened the gods, for each of the warriors fought like a hundred thousand men, — cut, slash! cut, slash! After fighting several hours, — for all the *oni* on our sacred islands came to the rescue of their friends, — the warriors despatched the last of the imps, and releasing the prisoners, recovered the treasure hidden in the cave and returned in triumph to Kioto, carrying the enormous head of Shu-ten-doji in procession through the streets."

(Bowing.) "Honorable sirs, such is the story of Raiko. Ah! in those good days Japan had brave men to kill the wicked demons that tormented the people." (Significantly.) "Now the red-headed *oni* torment us as they please and we have to suffer, for there is no one among us powerful enough to overcome them. Venerated be the memory of the immortal Raiko!"

"*Hai, hai*," approvingly murmured the audience.

I lingered until the last of his native patrons had retired, then inquired why he was so bitter against foreigners.

At first he protested that I was mistaken; but on discovering I understood the double meaning of his story, he frankly said, —

"Some of your countrymen come here with a new religion, which they assure us is better than ours; and others, rendered furious by the demon of drink, roam our streets day and night, and cruelly assault innocent persons. Why do you not, instead of inflicting your faith upon us, endeavor to convert your Shu-ten-doji? I beg that on your return to your honorable land you will explain this to your countrymen, and" (bowing low) " pardon the free tongue of an ignorant *hanashika*."

THE LEGEND OF LU-WEN, THE WOOD-CUTTER.

MANY of the most beautiful stories told by the *hanashika* are of Indian or Chinese origin, and are as old as the hills. Among the most popular and charming is the legend of Lu-wen, the wood-cutter, which bears such a striking resemblance to Irving's "Rip Van Winkle" that the latter appears to be a plagiarism of the Oriental tale. The following is the Japanese version:—

"The priests say, 'Pray continually: for every prayer uttered in this state you will escape a moment of pain in the next.' While this is well enough for persons who have nothing to do but to supplicate the gods, it is a bad doctrine to teach those who have families to support; in proof of which I will relate the story of Lu-wen, who, many centuries ago, dwelt in the shadow of the sacred mountain of Tendai, the highest peak of the Nanlin range [China].

"The wood-cutter, like most poor people, was blessed with many children, whose necessities compelled him to labor from daylight until dawn; notwithstanding which he was always cheerful, and contrived to keep the rice-pot well filled.

"One afternoon, while he was engaged in felling a tree, a begging priest interrupted him and inquired whether he had ever thought of a future state. The wood-cutter eyed the *bozu* askance, and curtly replied, —

"'I have no time to attend to such things. If you had to work for your living, as I do, and had a large family to support, you would not trouble yourself about the future. I find it hard enough to attend to the present. Please stand out of the way, or this tree may fall upon you.'

"The *bozu*, who had a 'golden tongue' and was used to hearing such plain talk, bowed and said, —

"'My son, you must not forget that you owe something to yourself. Every hour you devote to prayer will save you a hundred years' torture hereafter. Pray and work; then will your life be happy, and when the end of your present state approaches, you will close your eyes satisfied that you have attained one step toward eternal perfection. Think how terrible it would be to pass countless ages in various forms, each lower than the last, or to have your restless spirit wandering for millions of years amid the horrible labyrinths of hell. Would you suffer torments that no tongue can describe, thirst that even an ocean of water could not quench, hunger that no food could satisfy? Think of this, my son, and remember that for a present miserable outlay, a little self-sacrifice, and a few hours spent in holy contemplation, you may avert almost all these calamities, and will finally attain a seat on the sacred flower in the calm heaven of tranquillity and silence.'

"At first Lu-wen turned a deaf ear to his tempter's pleadings. However, being only a poor, ignorant fellow, he could not resist the sophistries of the learned man, who, after filling the wood-cutter's soul with apprehension, and emptying his pouch of the savings of a lifetime, retired, leaving the unhappy forester a prey to the most dismal forebodings.

"From that hour Lu-wen became a changed being, and instead of working with his axe, wasted his time in religious disputation with all who would listen to him, and in meditation and prayer.

"When winter came he would crouch over the scanty fire and count his beads, and during the rainy season he occupied the sheltered side of the hut, and compelled his children to stand in the puddles. Like all ascetics, he was mild of speech, inoffensive of manner, and willing to receive anything from anybody. As time rolled on his family increased, and their means of subsistence dwindled to nothing.

"At first his wife, who was an industrious, frugal woman, silently submitted to his eccentricities and turned a deaf ear to the advice of her neighbors, who did not fail to plainly express their opinions of her husband's conduct; but at last, unable to withstand the pitiful cries of her children, she determined to remonstrate with him. One morning, after he had dreamily swallowed the only food there was in the house, and was preparing to ascend the mountain in order to enjoy his devotions undisturbed, she approached him, prostrated herself, bowed respectfully, and murmured, —

"'I desire to say something important to you.'

"'Be quick,' he returned, 'do not worry me with your foolish gossip. I have my prayers to say.'

"This unkind reply stung her to the quick; and rising, she excitedly exclaimed, —

"'Honorable husband, listen to me. I can no longer contain my indignation, or bear the sight of our little ones' misery. Are you blind and deaf? Cannot you see that their stomachs are adhering to their backbones, and do you not hear them moaning for food? I have worked until my fingers are worn to the bone, and my strength is exhausted. I think it is time you again took your axe and did something more important than mumble prayers.'

"For a while he could not credit the evidence of his

ears; however, he presently recovered from his amazement, and replied sternly, —

"'Woman, the gods are before everything! Your words shock me! See, our children are listening, and will be led astray by your thoughtless expressions. You forget that I am known as the most pious man in this province.'

"'Pious! pious!' ejaculated the heart-broken creature, as she glanced around the miserable home and saw nothing but hungry faces and empty vessels. 'Your prayers do not fill our rice-pot!'

"'You are a vile creature!' he wrathfully answered. 'I will not waste my breath in endeavoring to change your nature. Consider yourself divorced. After this I will have none of you!'

"He snatched his axe from the corner where it had so long rested, and without deigning to look behind him, strode up the mountain-side, entered a mist cloud, and disappeared from her sight. As he vanished she dried her eyes, and indignantly exclaimed, —

"'You may go your way: I am satisfied. I would rather bear the stigma of divorce than struggle to support such a lazy, dreamy, good-for-nothing vagabond! May the foxes punish you for your unnatural behavior to your offspring!'

"Although the woman had in her anger expressed

the feelings that agitated her soul, she presently, like a true wife, began to reproach herself for having been so disrespectful to her husband; and when a neighbor looked in and inquired after her health, she sighed and replied, —

"'I fear I have driven Lu-wen away for good. Oh, what shall I do?'

"The visitor smiled, and glancing at her, said in a significant manner, —

"'Even ascetics must eat. Don't worry yourself: your husband will hurry back when he imagines he smells the burnt rice.'

"Lu-wen slowly ascended the mountain, and as he walked beheld the sun goddess drive back the dragon of the mist. Upon reaching his usual retreat, he seated himself on a shelf of rock and murmured a prayer. Overhead was the blue sky; behind him the glorious peak of Tendai, with its snowy crest glistening like a cone of silver; and at his feet the lovely valley, green with early rice and swarming with men and women busily engaged in cultivating the soil. The feathered pines gave out sweet odors, that, mingling with the perfume of ten thousand flowers, floated around him and charmed his senses; and as he listened to the song of the *peh-ling*, lark [called hundred-spirit bird], he smiled and said, —

"'What fools men are to toil and sweat in order to amass the dross of this earth! When will they learn that to acquire happiness it is only necessary to abandon material things and to pray to the gods? Here all is peace, and one is not tormented with the chatter of a woman's tongue.'

"Having thus expressed himself, he yielded to the soothing influences around him, and closing his eyes enjoyed the ecstasy of holy contemplation. While thus employed he heard a noise in the undergrowth, and arousing himself, saw a fox dart before him and vanish into a thicket of bamboo grass. Although not fond of hard work, he had a keen love of the chase; so he seized his axe, and rising, started nimbly in pursuit, thinking as he beat the covert, 'When the winter storms howl around the base of Tendai, it will be good to have a fox-skin to protect one's head.'

"He saw the creature's tail several times, but failed to run it down; and finally, after a prolonged chase, was about to give up the hunt and return to his devotions, when, entering a clear space, he to his amazement beheld two court ladies seated on a finely woven mat playing *sho-gi* [chess].

"The wood-cutter squatted respectfully, rested the head of his axe on the ground, and placing his chin on the but, watched the progress of the game, his soul being filled with a new emotion.

"'Ah!' he murmured to himself, 'if one of those glorious creatures would but notice me!'

"The pious Lu-wen, utterly forgetful of his good wife and starving children, continued to gaze upon the lovely ladies until the hours melted into days, the days into weeks, the weeks into months, the months into years, and the years into centuries; devoured by his passion and oblivious of all save its objects.

"The spring rains which saturated his decaying garments glanced harmlessly off the robes of his charmers, who neither heeded them, the sun of summer, nor the snows of winter, but played on 'as calmly as gods' a game that appeared endless.

"Lu-wen, utterly unconscious of the lapse of time and the changes that had taken place in his appearance, eagerly watched every move made by the mysterious ladies. After three hundred years he detected one of them in a false move, when he cried, 'Wrong, most beautiful woman!'

"In an instant the dames changed into foxes, and vanished among the brushwood; seeing which he thought, 'When the winter storms howl round the base of Tendai, it will be good to possess two fox-skins instead of one. I will secure them.'

"As he moved his chin from its resting-place, and rose to resume the chase, he discovered that his limbs were stiff; while the handle of his axe, which had been made of *kashi* [the hardest kind of wood], crumbled into punky fragments and scattered about his feet. With a tremendous effort he contrived to stand erect, when to his horror he found, in lieu of a shaven face, he possessed a flowing white beard, and that his head was covered with long, silvery hair.

"'Five hundred gods!' he cried, raising his hand and clutching his snowy locks. 'What has come over me? Ah, I understand! I have been bewitched by those foxes.'

"He passed his trembling fingers slowly over his wrinkled features, and glanced with a dazed expression at his withered limbs and time-worn garments; then, bent like a bow, hobbled down the mountain path.

"Although he easily found the main street of his native village, everything in it was changed. Saplings had grown into trees, the giant monsters that formerly shadowed the road were leafless and decayed, and he beheld new houses and strange faces; while the awed children, who peeped at him around the corners, whispered to one another, 'Who is that mountain spirit? Is he of the demons or of the ancient gods?'

"Presently he paused to rest, and shading his eyes with his palsied hands, quavered, 'How different everything is from what it was this morning!'

"After a while he reached the spot which had once been occupied by his hut, when he beheld an aged woman, who appeared to rise out of the ground, and who was as ragged and weird as himself. He alternately surveyed her and the wonder-stricken crowd that had gathered around them, then querulously demanded what had become of his home; adding, 'Surely I am not dreaming; this is the village of Yu-peen?'

"The crone regarded him with a penetrating glance, and replied, 'Yes, this is Yu-peen. What is your honorable name?'

"'I am Lu-wen, the wood-cutter,' he mumbled. 'This morning I quitted home, and ascended yonder mountain in order to pray undisturbed, and while thus employed was bewitched by foxes.'

"'This morning! this morning!' she cried. 'If you are Lu-wen, who left your wife and little ones to starve, you have been absent from here three hundred years.'

"'Three — hundred — years!' he gasped, placing his hands palm to palm in agony. 'Woman, surely you must be jesting!'

"'No, I speak the truth,' she bitterly replied. 'The gods, to punish you for neglecting your little ones, have prolonged your life until there is not a Lu-wen left to burn incense at your tomb.'

"Lu-wen led the way through the village past the old temple, the only building that he recognized, and entered the cemetery where rested the bones of his ancestors.

"The shadows of evening were falling, and the people followed the aged pair with awed faces and bated breath.

"Slowly, for the patriarch walked with great difficulty, the weird ones advanced until they arrived at the moss-covered tablets erected in memory of generations of Lu-wens, when the woman pointed significantly to a hillock, and said, 'There rest the bodies of your unfortunate children, who perished miserably through your piety.'

"As he gazed on the neglected graves, big tears coursed down his withered cheeks and moistened his snowy beard, and he covered his eyes with his hands as though he could not bear the sight. After a while he turned toward the tombs of his ancestors, prostrated himself, and for a few moments remained like one who is dead.

"The by-standers, pitying his age and infirmities, brought incense and assisted him to make his offerings; at the conclusion of which he rose, and addressing the people, said, —

"'My children, do not follow the advice of the *bozu*

when they tell you to pray continually. Prayer is good and the gods are merciful, but we must consider others as well as ourselves. For thinking solely of my own future I have been condemned to lose the happiest portion of my life, — my manhood. The foxes justly punished me for my inhuman behavior to my offspring. Remember my last words, — Work and pray. Farewell!'

"Thus speaking, he turned away sorrowfully and moved slowly in the direction of the mountain, followed at a respectful distance by the strange old woman, who, as he vanished into the gloaming, uttered a triumphant laugh and melted into air.

. . . .

"Although some unbelieving persons assert that the foregoing is merely an idle legend, invented by storytellers to frighten lazy persons who pretend to be pious in order to avoid labor, it is most certain that if you visit the mountain of Tendai when the moon is at its full, you will encounter the spirit of Lu-wen, the wood-cutter."

A JAPANESE DELICACY.

ON the street called Okiyo-koge (High Resting-Place of the Mikado), in Tokio, is a restaurant "where persons can enjoy the supreme delight of broiled eels." This establishment is kept by a man named Maroki, and is well worth a visit.

Most foreigners profess to dislike native food, and will not attempt to overcome their repugnance; while others boldly taste everything offered them, and soon learn to enjoy the perfect cookery and dainty service of the Japanese, and to prefer their dishes to the eternal sameness of our own.

One afternoon in April I was strolling about the streets, engaged in watching the interesting occupations of the people, when I met a young Japanese who had been educated at Harvard, and who appreciated a slice off the breast of a canvas-back duck and a tenderloin steak as perfectly as "one to the manor born." Having politely saluted me, he said, —

"I am on my way to Maroki's. Would you like to

join me in a feast of broiled eels? It is said that this month the *unagi* is a fit morsel for the gods."

"*Unagi?*" I replied, with a somewhat dubious shake of the head. "I never was very fond of those marine snakes."

"Probably you have never tasted them prepared by my countrymen," he slyly returned. "I remember once eating some at Delmonico's" (shuddering). "They were soft, flavorless morsels, enclosed in a quivering jelly. Come along with me and partake of a dish the taste of which will be pleasantly remembered long after you return to America. You, who are half a Japanese, ought not any longer to remain ignorant of one of our chief delicacies."

Summoning a *jin-riki-sha*, we squeezed into it in the economical native fashion, and after a brief ride turned into the Okiyo-koge *machi*, and alighted at the entrance to Maroki's establishment, — a two-story building, the lower apartment of which was furnished with grated, prison-like windows. In the entrance were the proprietor and his wife, who, as we paid our *jin-riki-sha* man, prostrated themselves, bowed their heads on the boards, and murmured, "Thousand welcomes to our humble place"; then, rising, awaited our pleasure.

"Are the eels good to-day?" patronizingly inquired my friend. "I have heard that their flavor is not quite what it used to be. Do you procure them from the city canals, or are they from the Sumida River?"

The proprietor again bowed, twitched the left corner of his mouth, after the fashion of a Japanese uttering a joke, and answered, —

"Honorable sir, do you for a moment imagine I would offer canal-bred eels to such a judge as yourself? No, no! you know that I have a high reputation, and buy nothing but the most beautiful fish that come from the Sumida. Remembering that the time was near for you to pay us a visit, I have saved some of my finest eels for you. Would you like to come into the kitchen and inspect them?"

"*Hai*," gently added his wife, who had listened to his speech with downcast eyes, "that is so. We have some *unagi* fit for a *daimio*."

"What do you say?" inquired my companion, turning to me. "Would you like to visit the culinary department?"

"Not until I have dined," I answered, sniffing suspiciously at the unmistakable odor of *daikon* (pickled radish) that issued from a rear apartment. "You know the old proverb, 'Do not make the acquaintance of the cook until the feast is over'? If I relish the eels, I may feel like learning how they are prepared for the table."

We slipped off our shoes and followed our hostess up a broad ladder to the floor above, which was divided by sliding screens of paper into a number of apartments. Here we were greeted by a score of chubby-faced, cherry-lipped, neatly dressed attendants, who knelt and welcomed us with profound bows.

"Which room do you prefer?" said the mistress. "This is not a busy hour, so most of the apartments are vacant."

My companion thought awhile, as though deciding an important matter; then haughtily replied, " We will occupy the one over the extension. I always feel at home there."

The woman led the way, and we entered a neatly matted room, about ten feet by twelve, the sole adornment of which were two *kakémono* (hanging pictures) representing Ebisu and Dai-koku, — gods of luck. Placing cushions on the floor, she invited us to seat ourselves upon them, prostrated herself, bowed gravely, and retired. In a few moments a black-eyed waitress, whose hair was polished like ebony and decorated with a single pin, entered with a *tabakobon* (box) containing live charcoal for our pipes. She deposited the apparatus on the floor between us, knelt, bowed, sat upon her heels, glanced modestly downward, and awaited our order.

My friend, who was what we term rather "airy," being a junior official in the foreign office, glanced patronizingly at the girl and said, —

"Bring us some trifles with which to amuse ourselves, then serve the broiled eels as fast as we require them. Mind, we don't want fish that have been cooked an hour. My guest is a gentleman who appreciates hot food. What wine have you on tap?"

The waitress, who, in spite of her drooping lashes and humble pose, was slyly watching me out of the corners of her eyes and laughing to herself at his affectation of importance, replied, —

"We have the *fuku-boten*, the *muso-ichi*, the *otari*, *yebisu-tai*, and the unrivalled *hanazakari*, which is the one I suppose your Exalted Excellency will order."

"Yes," he nodded. "Of course we want the most expensive. Bring us some *hanazakari:* I never drink such stuff as *fuku-boten*. Hurry up."

When she had retired I remarked, "Do you not notice a strange odor in this place? It makes me feel quite sick."

He sniffed once or twice in an unconcerned manner, lighted his pipe, blew the smoke through his nostrils, and regarding me with an amused expression, answered, —

"After you have been in Tokio as long as I have, you will be used to these trifles. I suppose you perceive the perfume which arises from the sewer outside the window. If you so desire, we will change to another room."

Upon my replying that I very much wished to do so, he summoned the attendant, who conducted us to an apartment overlooking the street, then retired for a few moments, and returned bearing two small trays containing little covered bowls and a bottle of the "flower in full bloom."

She knelt near us, filled two tiny cups with the *saké*, and proffered them to us, murmuring, "The wine is served."

As I sipped the delicious liquor I glanced at the pretty waitress, who was sitting on her heels, holding the bottle in her hand ready to replenish our cups.

"What is your name?" I asked.

"Kiku [chrysanthemum]."

"What food is there on this tray?"

She reached forward, and uncovering the bowls, said as she revealed their contents, "Sliced *daikon* [a rank-smelling radish], *niko-go-ri* [cakes of fish jelly], sliced raw *tai* [carp], ginger root, and seven kinds of vegetables."

"Please give me some *shoyu* [soy]."

Away she went, and soon was back with a red-lacquered tray, on which were two tiny, shallow saucers and a small teapot containing the sauce.

She served each of us with some of the relish, then again sat upon her heels and modestly cast down her eyes.

The *hashi* (chopsticks) of fragrant red cedar, resting on the trays, were unsplit at the top, showing they had never been used, and that the restaurant was a first-class one.

Taking up my pair I pulled them apart, and grasping them in the regulation fashion, proceeded to enjoy the food, my companion, who politely waited until I had tasted it, following my example.

The *daikon* was hot, hard, and salt, and I did not relish it; but the fish jelly, cakes, raw *tai*, and vegetables were exceedingly nice.

"These are only introductions to the real feast," remarked my friend. "Do not eat too freely, or you will be unable to enjoy the delicacy of the season."

When we had emptied the bowls, the waitress removed them, and quickly returned with some trays containing square black lacquered boxes, bearing the signs of the house and a number. Placing one before each of us, she removed the tightly fitting lids and revealed the contents, which were sections of nicely browned eels, skewered together, that gave out a most appetizing odor.

The girl smiled as she watched my looks, and replenishing my saucer with *shoyu*, placed it near me, murmuring, "I think you will find the *unagi* very pleasing to your taste."

I took my *hashi* in my right hand, inserted the points in the fish, broke off a morsel, and ate. Ye gods, it was delicious! rich, tender, delicately flavored, and boneless!

I drew my box toward me, nodded approvingly at the attendant, and enjoyed the delectable food.

The smiling girl brought in box after box, the contents of each being nicer than the last.

I have partaken of fried oysters at home, broiled fish in all countries, and the delicacies of every clime, but have never more thoroughly enjoyed any dish than I did those *unagi*.

At last I laid down my chopsticks, and glancing at my friend, exclaimed, "You were right in saying that this is a dish for the gods! We ought to introduce it in the States."

The waitress bowed in acknowledgment of my praise, and inquired if we would like some rice.

"Yes," nodded my companion, "I think I could empty a bowl or two."

The girl left us, and after a brief delay returned bearing a large tray, on which was a covered wooden tub containing hot rice, two lacquered bowls, a teapot, and some tiny cups.

I ate one portion of the delicious, well-cooked cereal; then lighted my pipe and watched my friend, who had his bowl refilled a dozen times, and who moistened his food by saturating it with tea.

"How do you contrive to render the skin of the fish so tender?" I asked the girl.

"I do not know," she answered, glancing timidly at the mats. "The cooks never permit us to learn their secrets. If you would like to visit the kitchen, they will no doubt explain everything to you."

"O Kiku, bring something to help us digest our food," said my companion. "I am afraid the eels will disagree with us."

The girl quitted the room and soon reappeared with a tray, on which was a lacquer cup containing some seeds of the *xanthouylon piperitum*, called by the Japanese *sancho*, which tastes like orange peel.

"Try those," he said; "if you feel any inconvenience from your dinner, they will quickly relieve you."

Not having emptied a tub of rice, I did not require the medicine. However, I asked the waitress if she would put up a few of the seeds for me to take home to the States.

"Now for the bill," said my companion, refilling his pipe. "Altogether you have given us a very tolerable meal"

In a few moments she came back, carrying a small scoop-like tray, in which was placed a slip of paper inscribed with the reckoning. She pushed this along the mat toward him, then bowed and remained with her face close to the floor, while he minutely scrutinized the document. Taking his purse from his sleeve, he dropped some paper money into the tray, and remarked in a low tone, "You may keep the change" (ten cents).

His munificence almost overpowered the waitress, who bowed repeatedly and murmured gratefully, "Your generosity resembles that of a foreigner. Any one can see that you have travelled."

After we had smoked awhile, he asked me whether I would like to visit the kitchen; and on my replying in the affirmative, summoned the landlady, who said, "You honor us too greatly"; offering me a small package, "Please accept this *sancho*"; adding, "My husband will show you how we prepare the eels."

We rose, quitted the room, and descending the ladder-like stairway, the steps of which were polished as smooth as glass, slipped on our foot coverings and entered the kitchen. On the hard earthen floor were rows of little charcoal furnaces, provided with iron rods that served as rests for the skewered eels. Maroki, who had a weakness for bowing and politely sucking in his breath between his speeches, led the way, and was exceedingly attentive. Pointing to a range of tubs containing fine specimens of *anguilla tenuirostrii*, he remarked, —

"These were caught this morning. They were the most expensive fish in the Nippon Bashi market. Are they not worth looking at?"

"How do you contrive to so completely extract their bones?" I demanded. "Our cooks cannot accomplish that feat."

He motioned to a lightly clad servant and said, "Some customers have just come in. Prepare an eel in the presence of these gentlemen."

The man, who evidently took great pride in his work, selected a vigorously squirming fish, struck its head smartly upon a wooden block placed upon the floor, and squatting by it, grasped the creature's neck, inserted a knife in the left side of the vertebræ, and dexterously ran it down to the tail; then rapidly applied his instrument to the other side of the backbone and repeated the process, leaving the eel split open. Holding up the head, to which were attached the vertebræ and lateral bones, enclosing the intestines, he bowed and said, "There is not a splinter left in the fish."

"That is so," proudly remarked the proprietor. "I only employ the most skilful men and cooks."

The operator washed down the block, chopped the flattened eel into three-inch lengths, and shouted to a cook, who advanced and removed it on a dish.

The next process was a mysterious one, and was performed behind a screen, from whence the platter of eels was handed out to one of the broilers. My opinion is that the fish had simply been plunged into boiling water, to make the skin tender.

We advanced to a range and saw a cook skewering the pieces of eel on long bamboo splints. Then he placed them on the rods over the glowing coals, and when one side was browned, dexterously picked them up with a pair of iron chopsticks and turned them. After they were thoroughly cooked, he seized the fish with the same instrument and plunged it into a vessel containing old *shoyu*, which was as thick and dark as molasses.

The steaming *unagi* were then drained, placed in a lacquer box, and sent up-stairs to the customer.

"We never prepare our eels until they are ordered," remarked the proprietor. "No matter how busy we may be, I will not have the fish killed beforehand."

"What do you do with the bones?" I asked.

"We boil them down into the delicious jelly you have already tasted. Nothing is wasted in this establishment. We think of the seven virtues."

I thanked him and gave the chief cook a gratuity. When we quitted the establishment, Maroki with his wife and the attendants were assembled in the entrance, bowing and exclaiming, "*Iro, iro arigato! Sayonara, sayonara!* [Many thanks! Farewell, farewell!]"

As we strolled up the street my companion said, "I hope you have enjoyed my poor entertainment."

"Yes," I responded. "I shall not soon forget Maroki's broiled eels; they are indeed a Japanese delicacy."

A LEGEND OF THE RAIN.

ONE afternoon in March, while I was seated on the matted floor of a friend's house in Sarugadai, in Tokio, chatting with the charming mother of my host, the rain suddenly began to patter upon the roof of the veranda; noticing which the old lady glanced into the garden, and said in a reflective tone, "To-day is the fifteenth of the month. Hush, little Umewaka is weeping."

Her observation puzzled me. However, I bowed respectfully and remarked in a complimentary manner, "What a difference there is between an American and a Japanese child! When our youngsters shed tears they generally howl at the top of their voices. Little Umewaka must be a model boy."

This speech quite overcame the studied politeness of my entertainer, who, after vainly endeavoring to refrain from smiling, laughed merrily and said, "Have you never heard the beautiful story of Umewaka-maru? I thought you were acquainted with all our legends."

"Oh, he is dead, is he?" I replied. "I understand: you spoke figuratively. I thought you were referring to one of your neighbors' children."

Her lips twitched, and she said, "To-day the anniversary commemorative service is held in the little temple at Muko-jima, on the left bank of the Sumida River. You and my son ought to visit the place. It is a very interesting spot."

As she concluded, my friend entered and said, "I have overheard my mother's suggestion. What do you say? shall we order our *jin-riki-sha?*"

Upon my acquiescing, he directed his servant to summon the conveyances, which were presently brought to the "mouth of the house."

Bidding my hostess adieu, I stepped into my carriage; and when I was seated, the *jin-riki-sha* man stooped, grasped the shafts, raised them breast high, and set off at a rapid pace, my companion being a short distance ahead.

The *jin-riki-sha* (man-power carriage) is a vehicle shaped like a baby wagon, and is usually roomy enough to accommodate two adults. It is drawn by one or more men, who are clad in tightly fitting blue cotton lower garments and short tunics of the same material, decorated with large white characters. These little, sturdy fellows earn from two to four dollars a week, for which sum they are expected to do the work of a horse, to act as a guide, drag from one hundred and fifty to three hundred pounds of humanity, to run from thirty to forty miles a day, and be sober, honest, good-humored, polite, and attentive to their patrons.

The shower was over, the sun was shining, and the keen, bracing air made our runners " feel good," so they rushed us along at a break-neck speed, turned the corners with a suddenness that almost deprived us of breath, ran helter-skelter down the steep hill of Saruga, and rattled us over the bridge of the canal; then, when their exuberant spirits were somewhat exhausted, settled down to a regular trot and began to thread the labyrinth of streets leading to our destination.

Most foreigners, upon first arriving in Japan, feel a repugnance to being trundled about in a vehicle drawn by a lightly clad human being; but the *jin-riki-sha* is so easy to enter and quit, and runs so pleasantly, that the novice soon overcomes his dislike and adopts the institution.

My runner was a lively fellow, who appeared desirous of showing how narrowly he could shave every obstacle in his way. Whenever he saw a woman with a child on her back nervously crossing the road, a hen or a dog enjoying the warm sunshine, or a coolie resting his heavy burden in our path, he would utter a savage whoop and charge right at them; then, when within an inch or two of his terrified victim, would suddenly swerve to the right or left, repeat his fierce cry, and continue upon his wild career.

As we were passing one of the gates of the Kaga Yashiki, an aged cat, lying in the road, rose, elevated its back, raised its stumpy tail, and spat at my man, who, unable to check his speed, ran his vehicle over the defiant animal. The poor creature uttered an agonizing *warro*, regained its feet, clambered up a stack of bamboos that rested against a neighboring house, and vanished; while my *jin-riki-sha-jin*, regardless of the owner's cries, kept right on, shouting, "*Hai, hai, hai!* [Get out of the way]."

A little farther on I beheld one of the vehicles of the Tokio Rapid Transportation Company bearing down upon us. It was a creaking, lumbering, dilapidated, condemned Broadway stage, drawn by two spavined horses, and driven by a wild-eyed, shock-headed youth, who cracked a long whip and loudly adjured his cadaverous animals. By his side sat a fat little ragamuffin armed with a tin horn, which he blew in a demoniacal fashion. The conveyance was tightly packed with lower-class Japanese, yelling as our country folks do when they are coming from camp meeting.

The driver noticed me, said something to the horn-blower, whipped up his sorry team, and charged right at us; noticing which, my runner responded with a fierce "*Hai-hai*," and deliberately collided with the skeletons. The frightened creatures shied, the man lashed them and swore in mingled pigeon English and Japanese, the passengers shrieked, and the spectators waited for the climax which soon came.

"*Yeh-yeh!*" snarled the coachman, sawing at the poor brutes' heads and vigorously plying his whip upon their trembling bodies. "*Yeh-bakka!*"

In another moment they were backing furiously; then the off wheels sank into a gutter, the axles snapped, the body of the stage toppled over and landed in an oil dealer's shop, and the animals, released from their burden, trotted off neighing joyfully.

My *jin-riki-sha* man, who had stopped to watch the result of his act, wiped his perspiring forehead and said in a comical aside, "People never get anything by running against me."

The scene that followed beggars description. The terrified passengers screamed, trembled with fear, prayed, and uttered imprecations; while the oil dealer and his shopman, who were hidden from view, vigorously boosted the obstacle, and finally moved it sufficiently to permit of their quitting the premises. Meanwhile the thieves gathered from all quarters and eagerly watched for an opportunity to ply their trade. After the last passenger had been rescued from the overturned stage, a policeman, wearing the inevitable spectacles, appeared from a neighboring station-house and made his presence known by belaboring some of the innocent by-standers, whose cries added to the infernal din.

At length the proprietor of the store advanced to the officer, and bowing respectfully, said, "Honorable official, what am I to do? Yonder carriage has no business in my shop. It is injuring my trade. Will you please order it to be removed?"

"Here, why don't you take your coach out of that?" blustered the policeman, addressing the crestfallen driver, who had just returned to the place, leading his runaway animals. "Are you aware that your employers will have to pay for your clumsiness?"

"Yes, that they will," pompously remarked the oilman, regarding the culprit severely. "In addition to the damage to my fixtures, my business is ruined for the day. I shall have a very long bill for the Tokio Rapid Transportation Company."

The coachman ruefully scratched his ear, and prostrating himself, said, "Honorable sirs, you are aiming at the wrong object"; then, rising, scowled ferociously, and pointing at me, cried, "He did it! He did it!" On hearing this speech, my runner stepped between the shafts of my vehicle, picked them up, and started at a rapid pace, shouting, "*Hai, hai, hai!*"

In vain the policeman yelled at us to stop: my man was deaf to his commands, and threaded in and out the gaping crowd until we were at a safe distance, when he halted, and regarding me slyly, murmured, "This sort of work makes one very thirsty." I gave him a few *cash,* and when he had refreshed himself, he resumed his place in the shafts and ran as nimbly as ever.

I did not rejoin my friend before we reached the approach to the Ogawa-bashi, a broad, well-built bridge over the Sumida River. After crossing the structure, we alighted and entered an avenue of cherry-trees ruddy with the rising sap. As we walked slowly along the bank of the river, which was alive with men and boys angling for minute fish, my companion halted, and pointing to one of the trees, said, "When I look at the red bark of the *sakura* [cherry], I remember the beautiful poem written by Kojima: —

>[" '*Ten Kosen wo horobosu nakare*
>*Toki ni Hanrei naki ni shimo aradzu.*
>
>[O Heaven! destroy not Kosen,
>While Hanrei still lives.' "] *

---

* This translation is quoted from "The Mikado's Empire," by Prof. W. E. Griffis.

He uttered the foregoing in the monotonous singsong affected by the Japanese when repeating poetry, and covertly alluded to the approach of spring; though a foreigner, ignorant of the peculiarities of Japanese thought, would have been greatly puzzled to understand the double meaning of the stanza.

At the end of the long avenue we found the little temple, the object of our pilgrimage, which was crowded with women, who were listening attentively to the droning of some shaven-headed *bozu* (priests). Finding it impossible to enter the building, we retired to a neighboring *chaya* (tea-house) and ordered refreshments. While we were enjoying ourselves, a travelling *saimon* (begging story-teller), holding in his hand a wooden instrument which he jingled like a sleigh-bell, approached us, knelt, bowed his head to the ground, and said, "Honorable gentlemen, would you like to hear the beautiful story of Umewaka's tears?"

"Yes," I replied; "but do not collect a crowd. We will pay you for your entertainment."

"You had better ask him in," said my companion. "If he remains outside he will soon attract people; for he cannot refrain from using his clapper."

I followed this suggestion, and invited the *saimon* to enter. At first the vagabond pretended to be too bashful; however, he presently arose, stepped into the room, squatted at the regulation distance from us, bowed respectfully, and commenced his story: —

"What is stronger than a mother's love? Though demons may part a woman from her son, she will search for him everywhere. The gods blessed women by implanting maternal affection in their hearts. Every one should pay respect to the honorable mother.

"The *sakura* shading the mansion of Yoshida-no-sho-sho, in Kioto, were in full bloom, and the moon-goddess was illuminating them with her silvery light. The attendants of little Umewaka-maru, attracted by the glorious scene, had one by one quitted their posts, and he was left alone. Stealthily as a tiger advances upon its prey, a masked figure, nude as a wrestler, enters the apartment. Is it an *oni* [ghoul], a demon from another world, or one of those wretches who torture the hearts of parents by stealing children? Alas! it is a *kado-mukashi* [kidnapper].

"The fiend moves warily, pauses frequently, listens anxiously to the murmur of the voices in the garden, creeps onward and stoops; then, placing his right hand over the mouth of the sleeping boy, inserts his left beneath the child's body, raises him in his arms, once more listens with breathless attention, and vanishes.

"The time passed so pleasantly that the attendants forgot all about their duty, and it was not until the temple-bell sounded the hour of the ox [2 A. M.], and the moon was retiring behind a bank of clouds, that they remembered their young master, and returned to resume their watch over him. As they reached the apartment they beheld his mother, who had been awakened from her sleep by a terrible dream, and who, after surveying the empty bed, inquired, 'Where is my son? Wretches, what have you done with him?'

"Although they searched every nook and corner of the house and grounds, they failed to discover the boy, and from that hour never again beheld him.

"His mother, rendered frantic by grief, cut off her hair, and assuming the garb of a nun, roamed from province to province, eagerly seeking for her lost darling. Meanwhile the poor boy was carried to the North, and subjected to the most cruel treatment.

"One night a party of men, accompanied by a lad about thirteen years old, arrived on yonder spot" (pointing to the little temple at the end of the avenue). "They were loud of voice, savage of aspect, and continually urged him to quicken his steps.

"'Honorable sirs,' he faintly pleaded, 'I am too weary to go any farther. I pray you to let me rest awhile, or my spirit will depart from my body.'

"This speech enraged the wretches, who replied to his prayer with kicks and blows, and left him in a ditch to die.

"When they were out of sight he contrived to clap his hands twice to summon the *kami* [gods], whom he thus addressed: —

"'Host of deities, give ear to my humble petition. In consequence of heavy crimes committed in a former state, I am justly punished in this. Still, gods of the high celestial plains, I beseech you to have pity upon my youth and misery, and to let me once more behold the face of my honored mother.'

"Then he became unconscious, and the *kami* mercifully sent an old farmer to his aid. This good man, whose features were knotted like the roots of a bamboo, had dreamed that he saw the boy in the ditch, and on awakening had taken his lantern, and gone to learn if the gods had visited him in his sleep. On seeing Umewaka he wept and said, —

"'What demons some people are! This poor child doubtless has a father and mother; he has apparently been the victim of kidnappers. I will do my best to succor him.'

"The dying child wearily opened his eyes, and gazing at the farmer, pitifully exclaimed, 'Oh, spare me; I cannot rise! Indeed, indeed, I am not pretending! Oh, do not strike me again!'

"'Merciful Buddha! this is shocking!' sobbed the aged man, kneeling and placing his arm under the sufferer's head. 'Fear not, my son: though I am only a poor farmer, I have enough for you and myself. I will adopt you, and treat you well. Be comforted: the good hour has come.'

"As he spoke the tears trickled down his rugged cheeks, and fell upon the features of Umewaka. The latter, somewhat revived by the kind words, regarded his new friend and said,—

"'Listen, honorable sir: the thread of my existence will soon be snapped, and before it parts I have much to say. Though clad in rags, I am Umewaka, the son of Yoshida-no-sho-sho of Kioto. I pray you will communicate with my parents, and tell them of my sad fate.'

"'I swear to do all you wish,' huskily replied the good man. 'Have you any other commands for me?'

"'Yes, yes,' feebly responded Umewaka. 'Bury me in this spot, and plant a *yanagi* [willow] over my grave, which will show my honorable mother that I am always weeping for her'; adding, '*Yanagi no yeda ni uki orewa nashi!* [The snow does not break the branches of the willow].'"

The *saimon* paused and sounded his clapper from force of habit, when my friend testily remarked, "Go on, go on! You will get your pay in a lump, after your narrative is finished."

The story-teller regarded us slyly and murmured, "The close atmosphere of this apartment has produced a painful dryness in my throat. I have heard that *saké* [wine] is a good thing for such a complaint."

I ordered the refreshment to be brought him; and when he had partaken of several cups, he continued:—

"The farmer bowed respectfully, and said to the dying boy, 'Honorable master, rest assured that your command shall be obeyed. I will select a vigorous young tree, and choose an auspicious day for planting it. While I go to seek your honorable parents, my neighbors will watch your grave, and see that no evil insect attacks the *yanagi*.'

"Umewaka endeavored to reply, but his strength failed him. In a few moments he sighed gently and closed his eyes, and the thread of his existence was snapped in twain. The good old man faithfully kept his promise, and after performing the proper ceremonies, set out for Kioto.

"On arriving at the house of Yoshida-no-sho-sho, he discovered that its mistress was absent; and as no one could tell whither she had gone, he returned to this place and resumed his usual occupation.

"The willow grew miraculously, and within a few months attained a great height, and had beautiful pendulous branches, the rustling of which was asserted by the villagers to resemble the words *okka-san* [mother].

"On the 15th of March, the anniversary of Umewaka's death, while the farmer and his neighbors were weeping over the simple grave, a lady dressed in a religious garb approached the group, and after watching them for a while said, 'My soul is strangely agitated. I beg you will tell me for whom you are mourning.'

"The aged mán bowed and answered, 'For Umewaka-maru, the son of Yoshida-no-sho-sho.'

"On hearing this the nun swooned, and remained unconscious until nightfall, when she begged the people to leave her to commune with the spirit of her child.

"At the hour of the rat [midnight], Umewaka-maru appeared and saluted her respectfully, saying, 'Honorable mother, my tears have not been shed in vain. For a year my soul has inhabited this tree. The merciful *kami* have heard my prayer, and sent vou to this spot.'

"The trembling lady clasped her hands palm to palm and said, 'I have wandered thousands of miles; my feet have been cut by the sharp rocks of the mountain, and lacerated by the thorns of the forest. I have suffered the pangs of hunger and thirst, and have travelled by day and night searching everywhere for you, and hoping to behold you in this life. Although the gods have denied my prayer, I feel happy at being permitted to see you thus. What can I do to give your wearied soul rest?'

"'Pray with me to the *kami*. Now that they have granted my desire, they will doubtless mercifully release me from my present state.'

"Spirit and mortal then prostrated themselves, and remained for some hours silently petitioning the immortals.

"As the day dawned the beloved form vanished, and the lady beheld only the weeping *yanagi*, the branches of which, agitated by the morning breeze, seemed to murmur, *Okka-san! Okka-san!*'

"She caused yonder temple to be erected to the memory of Umewaka, and bequeathed money for the annual celebration of a service in his memory. It is said that when her spirit quitted her body it assumed the form of a white stork, which returns every year and listens to the prayers offered for the repose of her son's soul."

The *saimon* paused, solemnly rattled his clapper, and added, "When it rains on the 15th of March, the people say, 'Hush! little Umewaka is weeping.'"

STREET SCENES IN TOKIO.

OF the many novel objects in the wonderful city of Tokio, none are more interesting to the foreigner than the people who earn their living on the streets. These industrious creatures come and go at stated periods, have their regular haunts, attract attention by their peculiar dresses and strange cries, and play an important part in the comedy of city life.

At dawn, long before the shopkeepers have quitted their mats, the *kami-kudzu-hiori* (paper scrap collector) emerges from his squalid hut and commences his rounds. He is usually an old, old man, clad in patches and shreds, and wears a very broad-brimmed reed hat, while for sanitary or other reasons his nose and mouth are covered with a ragged blue towel. Upon his left side he carries a huge but light basket, and in his right hand two long bamboo rods, used like tongs. He seldom speaks to any one, goes about his work in a systematic manner, and is to Tokio what the rag-picker is to New York; though, unlike his foreign brother, he generally confines himself to the collection of waste paper, not a scrap of which escapes his ferret-like eyes.

Having formerly belonged to the despised Eta class, he is very humble, and from force of habit bows to all the well-dressed persons he encounters. As he silently moves along the street he carefully turns over every little pile of rubbish with his sticks, picks out the pieces of paper, and jerks them into his capacious receptacle. It is wonderful how dexterously he handles the instruments: one moment using them to tear a fluttering fragment of placard from a fence, and the next inserting them between the bars of a window and filching a book carelessly left in sight by its owner. He is a wary, thievish old rascal, and many a boy's kite and servant-girl's novel that have mysteriously disappeared from the house have found their way into his basket. In addition to having a bad reputation for appropriating all kinds of paper, he is said to be a dog-stealer. Apropos of this I will relate a somewhat amusing incident.

One morning, having risen earlier than usual, I took my seat by the grated window of my chamber and watched the passers. Presently a gentle-faced old lady, followed by a dog, came in sight, and encountering a friend, bowed low and began an animated conversation. While they were thus employed a *kami-kudzu-hiori* stealthily approached her from behind, and after striking the dog upon the head, picked up the insensible creature with his sticks, threw it into his basket and covered it with the contents, then coolly proceeded to examine some rubbish deposited by the wayside. The old lady soon missed her pet and began to call for him; meanwhile the paper collector continued his occupation in an unconcerned manner, as though guiltless of the theft.

"Have you seen my beautiful little dog?" inquired the woman, regarding him suspiciously.

"Dog, dog?" he answered, bowing servilely. "Honorable lady, do you take me for a thief?"

"Yes; I believe you have stolen him," she indignantly replied. "I suppose you want to make a few *cash* by turning his beautiful skin into a drumhead."

"Honorable lady, indeed you are mistaken," murmured the rascal, shifting his basket on to his back, crouching to the ground, and bowing his head. "It is true, I am only a miserable *kami-kudzu-hiori;* still, I am strictly honest. I have not set eyes upon your amiable animal. If you will describe him and tell me where you live, I may meet him in my walks, when I will restore him to you."

"My little Chin has a black-and-white coat, and he wears a red-and-yellow cotton frill round his neck. Although you pretend to be so simple, I believe you know something about him."

"The gods will bear witness to my innocence," murmured the rascal, with his face close to the ground. "It is hard enough to be poor without being charged with dishonesty."

While he was speaking the animal recovered its senses, wriggled from beneath the paper scraps, leaped upon the thief's back and barked at his overjoyed mistress, who, taking him in her arms, uttered shrill cries of "Police!"

The *kami-kudzu-hiori* rose hurriedly and was darting off, when he ran into the arms of a long-haired, spectacled policeman, who was clad in a tight blue foreign uniform, and who had been attracted by the woman's cries. The officer clubbed the fellow until he ceased to offer resistance, then sternly inquired what the man had done, and on learning the truth, marched the offender to the police office. The ladies followed, scolding the thief at the top of their voices, and as they went, explaining his crime to the passers-by.

Though the *kami-kudzu-hiori* have a bad reputation and are objects of scorn, many of them are honest fellows, who work from dawn to dusk to earn the pitiful amount they receive for their collections. When they have filled their baskets they proceed to the dealer in waste paper, who is, compared with them, a man of wealth, and who treats them in a haughty and disdainful manner, often saying, "I have no use for such rubbish as you have brought me. Why don't you secure something really valuable?"

The ragged wretch bows, and exhibiting the contents of his basket, replies, "You are mistaken. I have here a very fine lot of paper. Please weigh it and give me my money."

After squabbling over the price, the dealer produces a wooden balance, inserts the hook in the basket, raises it from the ground, moves the stone weight along the yard, and gravely announces the number of *kin* (about one pound and three quarters).

The decision is usually disputed by the seller, who utters piteous outcries and vows that the man is robbing him. Finally, when they come to terms, the tradesman takes up his *soroban* (counting-board), and after making a calculation with the beads, draws a money-bag from his sleeve and drops a few copper *rin* (mills) into the trembling hands of his customer. The latter then carefully counts and examines every coin; having done which he bows low, rises, slings his basket over his back, and resumes his weary round.

As the sun peeps over the housetops the tradesmen begin to take down the shutters of their stores, and the tortoise-sellers, pipe-menders, candy-makers, and peripatetic venders appear upon the streets.

The dealer in objects of natural history squats on the

ground behind some tubs containing goldfish and little tortoises; above the vessels being a sort of bamboo gallows, from which are suspended a number of the patient reptiles, that move their clawed feet and wave their horny tails in a most helpless fashion. He is generally an inoffensive, middle-aged individual, — with peculiar ideas on the subject of zoology, for he will gravely assure his customers that his leather-backed stock will, if properly treated, attain the age of a thousand years, and that the possession of one of the stupid creatures will insure long life and happiness.

The pipe-mender does not remain any length of time in one place, but moves from street to street, carrying his tools in a long, narrow box that serves him for a bench. He takes his stand in some convenient nook apart from the crowd and utters a series of howls, which persons profoundly versed in Japanese translate as follows: "Old pipes made new again."

His patrons, who are of the poorest class, bring him dilapidated specimens of the tiny-bowled smoking instruments, and haggle about the price he asks for his works.

After carefully examining a worn pipe, the bamboo stem of which requires renewing, he will say to the owner, "My charge for replacing this old stick with an elegant new one is only five *rin*."

"Five *rin!*" screams his patron. "Do you think I am made of money? I can go into the country and cut all the pipe-stems I want. I do not intend you shall make your day's rice out of me. The old tube will last yet awhile."

The mechanic utters an exclamation of disgust, and responds satirically, "I suppose you expect me to mend your pipe for nothing. I do not steal my bamboos, like some people."

This retort, which is highly relished by the crowd, turns the laugh against the customer, who haughtily replies, "Go on with your work! I will find you in food for the next week or two."

The operator takes a tiny hammer and removes the bowl and mouthpiece of the pipe; then, selecting a bamboo, proceeds to fit it, carefully saving the rejected stick and the fragments that he saws from the new one to help boil his rice-pot at night. He is at infinite pains to make the joints air-tight, and as he works, delivers a comical lecture to the admiring crowd collected about him.

"See the wisdom that animates the owner of this pipe! Some men would have thrown it aside or disposed of it to a second-hand dealer" (closing one eye and looking down the stem to ascertain if it were straight). "For the pitiful sum of five *rin*, I have renewed the beauty of this useful instrument" (taking out a piece of soft paper and a little powder, and polishing the mouthpiece). "The economical gentleman has a soul full of wisdom; still, one can be too saving. For instance, if you have an old pipe and the artist who repairs it demands five *rin* for his labor, it is meanness to offer him four, because he will only give you an inferior stem that will crack and will not last a day."

Then, grimacing at the spectators and politely bowing and handing the pipe to his customer, he adds, "I ought to charge you ten *rin* for this excellent piece of workmanship. However, I always keep my agreement, so will be content with what you have promised. Five *rin*, if you please."

Japanese children, like our own, are very fond of sweets, and the stands of the *moji-yaki* (literally "letter burners") and *ameya* (modellers of rice extract), and the little canopied wagons of the masked *kompeito* (candy) pedlers, are always surrounded by eager crowds of boys and girls.

The *moji-yaki* is a great favorite with the youngsters, who watch his actions with dilated eyes. He is usually seated in a recess between two houses, behind a portable counter on which are placed a small bowl of live charcoal, some little copper griddles, and a vessel filled with thick sirup. He generally knows the names of all his patrons, whom he addresses after the following fashion: —

"*Hai-yaku-hai!* [Hundred bows, — a respectful form of salutation.] Honorable master boys, my bosom opens as I once more behold your faces. You all know I am the only man in Tokio who can make a sugar fish lifelike enough to deceive the *kawasemi* [kingfisher]. Now produce your money and I will begin my manufacture."

Having secured a customer, he places one of his griddles upon the glowing embers, and proceeds to pour some of the liquid sugar upon it; then taking the handle, runs the melted mass evenly upon the mould, and dabs it with patches of brilliant color. When it is crisp, he dexterously peels off the candied figure, fastens it to a splinter of bamboo, and hands it to his customer, saying, "Taro" (or "O Momo"), "you know a good article when you see it. One *rin*. Thank you. Who is my next honorable customer?"

The *ameya* is a more accomplished individual than the "letter burner," he combining modelling with painting. Like his brother artist, he occupies a small bench, over which is erected a bamboo frame for the exhibition of his manufactures, while the lower part is furnished with drawers containing his stock in trade. He is usually a shrewd old man who has failed in business, and taken to the trade of *ameya*, which requires very little capital. After singing a short ditty to collect the children, he smiles benevolently, bows, and says, —

"Tell me what I can do for you. Give me something really difficult to make. I am tired of modelling ducks and frogs. Don't be bashful, or expect that I shall empty your purses: I only charge two *rin* each for my wares."

"Please make me a monkey hanging from a tree," timidly requests a brown-cheeked little fellow, blushing at his own forwardness.

The *ameya* thinks for a moment, blinks his eyes merrily, and replies, "Oh, that is too easy! Give me a task that will enable me to display my ability."

"Two monkeys," suggests a little girl, who carries a great baby on her back, and whose complexion is completely hidden with bismuth.

"You are not paying for this, miss," he answers sharply, taking a bamboo tube and dipping it into some thick, opaque rice gluten. "Master Taro ordered me to make one monkey; if you want two, I will attend to you as soon as I have complied with his wishes."

He applies the other end of the bamboo to his mouth, dilates his cheeks, and inflates the viscid substance. The little ones anxiously watch him, and as the soft mass swells, he punches it here and there, dexterously pulls out and models the arms, and presently produces a very good representation of a monkey; seeing which the children shout gleefully, and the one who has given the order holds out his hand for the prize.

"One moment, my fat little master," cries the *ameya*, transferring the soft figure to a little stick, to which it clings in a very lifelike manner. "Let me complete my work."

He smiles blandly, takes a number of brushes from a drawer in the stand, inserts them between his fingers, and charges their points with color. In a few seconds the animal's face is adorned with a pair of goggle-eyes; blue bars are painted to indicate its nose, a red line is added for the grinning mouth, and the paws and feet are developed with streaks of black. Then the old fellow exhibits it triumphantly, and exclaims, "Master boy, I advise you to be very cautious not to tease this, or it may bite you." (Handing it to the little fellow.) "Take my advice: kill the *saru* [monkey], and eat it at once; then you will become as big and strong as a wrestler."

After receiving his fee, he turns to the other children and says, "What shall I make next? A mouse nibbling a *daikon* [radish], a string of rats chasing one another, or a gourd for your father's *saké* [wine]?"

Although I have often watched the *ameya*, I never saw his customers eat their purchases; but I have been told that the children, after keeping the pasty-looking, highly colored figures until they become hard, devour them with the greatest satisfaction.

The *kompeito* seller, who is not a manufacturer, attracts his customers by wearing a grotesque white mask representing the head of a god Fox. He is also provided with a small *taiko* (drum), which he beats continuously, as he does so singing a short stanza in praise of the deity who watches over the safety of the city. His stock in trade consists of the *kompeito* (little candies covered with spine-like protuberances, and flavored with peppermint, ginger, and an essential oil that tastes like wintergreen), burnt peas and beans coated with suger, lozenges and cakes of bean-flour, and a brilliant array of candies, the names of which are only known to Japanese children. Each kind is exposed in a neatly made box, and the collection is carried in a little wagon, with a tent-like roof of paper, the sides of the vehicle being furnished with screens of split bamboo to protect the delicacies from thieves. He moves all over the city, but has regular hours for visiting certain places, where he halts, beats his tambour, lowers his mask, executes a sort of break-down, and repeats his song in praise of the god Fox, which brings the *rin* from the sleeves of the mothers and enables him to gain a good living.

The foregoing describes only a few of the many quaint objects that may any day be seen upon the streets of Tokio.

A VISIT TO A JAPANESE THEATRE.

WHEN a Japanese gentleman visits the theatre, he does not purchase tickets at the box office, but proceeds to a neighboring *chaya* (tea-house), the proprietor of which selects the seats required by his patron, escorts him to the temple of the drama, takes care of his sandals, and during the entertainment furnishes him with refreshments.

Early one morning in May, I went with some friends to see the performance at a second-class *shibai* (theatre) in Asakusa. The street was thronged with pleasure seekers out for the day, and contained more than one place of amusement, the employés of which eagerly solicited the crowd and loudly vaunted the superiority of their respective establishments.

We entered a *chaya*, ascended to the upper floor, and summoning the host, inquired which company was the best, and the names and natures of the plays.

The man bowed respectfully, politely sucked in his breath, and replied, "The theatre over the way has no rival in the world. It is conducted by persons of great ability, who employ only the very highest order of talent.

You have arrived upon an auspicious day, and will witness the performance of two first-class pieces. I can guarantee you the most comfortable seats in the house."

We ordered tea, bade the man secure two boxes for us, and while he was gone watched the scene on the street. The front of the theatre was covered with large framed pictures, representing terrible scenes of bloodshed; and ranged over the shed-like projections of the wide entrances were a number of grotesque life-size portraits of the leading members of the troupe. On the right was the gallery ticket office; in the centre, one for the persons who paid the second price and had seats on the floor of the house; and upon the left — the place of honor — were sold the billets for the boxes.

After we had enjoyed the tea, our host returned and said, "This way, honorable gentlemen: the *maye-kio-gen* [opening dance] is about to begin."

Descending the stairs, we quitted the *chaya* and followed the man across the road into the theatre; then ascended the matted, stair-like ladder and were conducted along a narrow corridor. When about midway, our guide pushed two sliding doors aside, and bowing, said, "Honorable sirs, these are your places. See, they are provided with elegant cushions and cloths to protect your clothes from dust. Shall I bring you tea or *saké?*"

We gave our orders and proceeded to squat upon the

floors of the *sajiki* (boxes), which were nothing more than sections of the first balcony, separated by low rails. The "gods" occupied the *shikifune*, a raised gallery behind the central row of boxes facing the stage, and in the same part of the house was an enclosed space reserved for the officials of the theatre.

The *udzura* (floor of the building) was divided into compartments, in which squatted the middle class of patrons, and which was intersected by two broad platforms, extending from the entrance to the stage, termed *hana-michi* (flower paths). The building, above the first floor, was open at the sides; the absence of windows rendering the ventilation perfect, and admitting numerous "dead-heads" in the shape of swallows, doves, and butterflies. None of the woodwork was painted, and the interior had an ancient, cobwebbed, bare look, that contrasted strongly with the gaudy picture on the *maku* (curtain) veiling the stage, which represented a branch of cherry blossoms and bore the following inscription:—

"Presented by Narita Nurigome, who sells unrivalled *saké* near this theatre."

Every temple of the drama has a number of such curtains, furnished by tradesmen as advertisements for their wares, it being understood that the gifts shall be exposed at least once during every performance.

After we were comfortably seated, the *geza* (orchestra), which was partly hidden from view in a hut-like, barred structure on the left of the proscenium, frantically began its wild performance. The flutes tooted, the *sho* wailed, the *samisen* twanged, the *kokiu* (three-stringed violins) squeaked, and the drums rumbled. Meanwhile the spectators smoked, chatted at the top of their voices, and shouted derisively to new comers who were anxiously searching for friends among the sea of faces.

About eight o'clock the *maku* concealing the stage was drawn aside, and we beheld a box scene representing the interior of a tea-house. The central portion rested on a turn-table, level with the rest of the platform; the wings did not extend as high as the drops, and there was only one of the latter.

The audience murmured approvingly and eagerly scanned the scene; then the *to-dori* (living play-bill) advanced to the footlights and announced the title of the drama and names of the actors. When he had retired, a party of men dressed as the "Seven Lucky Ones" bounded upon the stage and danced the *maye-kio-gen*, which greatly delighted my friends; though I soon grew tired of it and felt glad when the grotesque beings made their exit, and the play was commenced by the entrance of a young *samurai* (gentleman) followed by a *geisha* (singing girl). The youth was blind and was desperately in love with the girl, who also had an admirer of an humbler order. A very excruciating love scene followed, in which the actors hugged themselves instead of one another, and the girl frequently veiled her features with her sleeves and wept.

During the entire performance *kurumbo* (boys clad in black robes, with hoods like those worn by the Inquisitors) attended upon the actors and arranged their dresses, then retired on all fours up the stage and squatted like monkeys with their backs to the audience, who were supposed not to be cognizant of their presence. It was very comical to see the imps crawling about and handing the leading people their pipes, etc. The action of the play was as follows: —

The blind *samurai* (gentleman) promises to marry the *geisha* (singing girl). The heavy villain, her lover, who is a gambler, finding that he is about to lose his sweetheart, determines to rob the *samurai's* house and to kill him. The stage revolves, new wings are pushed forward, and we behold a garden and the outside of a mansion with the moon shining upon the scene. The girl's lover enters silently, accompanied by his wild-eyed comrades. They indulge in long, bombastic asides and much pantomime, indicative of what they intend to do; then stealthily approach one of the paper windows of the dwelling, push it aside, crawl in and make their exits to delirious music, expressive of murderous designs. A crash is heard inside the house, then a succession of dull thuds, and one after the other the "bold, bad men" are artistically "fired" back into the garden. As the last of the robbers falls sprawling upon the stage, the blind *samurai* appears in the opening and delivers a speech out of the right corner of his mouth, describing how he was awakened by his assailants, and how he had "clubbed the crowd" with a weapon that belonged to his honorable deceased father. He steps down upon the stage, pirouettes, and defies unseen enemies to tread on the hem of his *kimono*. Meanwhile the robbers recover their senses and retire, menacing him in pantomime. Enter *geisha* tinkling her guitar. Blind *samurai* pauses and listens.

"Ah! 'tis my beloved O Cho-cho [Miss Butterfly]."

Another love passage ensues, he speaking tenderly out of the left corner of his mouth, and amorously clasping his arms, and she responding in a shrill falsetto, and significantly hugging her guitar, while the orchestra indulges in Wagner-like strains. Naughty *geisha* leads the confiding *samurai* towards a pillar-like stone lantern, bids him a tearful farewell, gives a signal to her lover, and retires, waddling like a duck. Orchestra executes more savage music. Re-enter heavy villain followed by a fresh detachment of assassins, who silently surround the brave youth. The act now rapidly approaches its climax; the audience listens with breathless interest, and gazes fixedly at the performance. Though the gallant *samurai* is hedged in with glittering, naked weapons, he defiantly utters a long speech that causes the lady patrons to sob and rock themselves, and the men to murmur and suck in their breath approvingly. Suddenly he draws his sword, twirls upon his toes, delivers blows with lightning rapidity, and severs limbs with a dexterity amazing to behold. Heads fly about like cannon balls and land in extraordinary places. One drops on the top of the *toro* (stone lantern), where it continues to wink and blink at the spectators; another falls on the summit of a post and rolls its eyes ferociously at its conqueror. The stage is smothered with blood, and soon all the assailants are *hors de combat*. Then the girl re-enters, coolly surveys the remains, and makes a speech of about fifteen lines, in which she laments having attempted to betray such a brave *samurai*. The latter struts up and down the "flower paths" and exhibits his costume to the admiring maidens among the audience, who devour him with their glances. At the conclusion of the *geisha's* speech he stamps alternately with his right and left foot and shouts ferociously:—

"*Yeh! yeh!* I hear a voice."

Naughty *geisha* cowers and trembles until the boards vibrate beneath her. Young *samurai*, who is still full of fight, imagines that she is one of his assailants and rushes upon her. In despair she utters his name; too late! The keen blade is thrust,— under her left arm; she falls Tableau. He discovers who she is, hugs himself, sobs passionately, tears round the stage to the wildest music that ever tortured human ears; withdraws the sword from the costume of the prostrate *geisha;* poses dramatically, rolls his sightless orbs, "speaks a piece" occupying about thirty minutes in its delivery, stabs himself, and expires "like a little man." The black demons then advance with large cloths, which they hold before the bodies of the slain, while the latter make their exits on all fours, and the orchestra indulges in low, wailing sounds, descriptive of deep woe. The stage is cleared, and the young *samurai* and girl, miraculously restored to life, figure prominently in five more acts, after which they commit suicide, presumably on account of having had too much of each other's society.

The acting was most excellent, and, notwithstanding the absence of plot, the piece was a great hit, moving the audience to tears and laughter, and often causing them to shout, "*Yerai*" (wonderful) and "*Nipon-ichi*" (literally, first-rate Japanese).

Between each act a different *maku* [curtain] was exhibited, and at the conclusion of the drama a gorgeously decorated screen was drawn before the stage, on which signal the people in the body of the house produced their picnic boxes and lighted their pipes, and the proprietor of our *chaya* entered, followed by his servants bearing trays of refreshments.

"Would you like to go round and inspect the stage?" he asked politely. "The proprietors are my very good friends, and I can take you over any part of the house."

We accepted his offer, and, having eaten our luncheon, accompanied him behind the scenes, where we were received by the managers, who, after bowing and sucking in their breath, led the way below.

The circular portion of the stage was pivoted, and its outer edge rested on a groove filled with well-greased, wooden balls. At a signal from one of the officials, twelve nude men grasped the tie-pieces and, bending nearly double, caused the platform to revolve slowly.

We returned to the upper world and inspected the property-room and its contents, then were conducted up-stairs and introduced to the *za-gashira* (star). On learning that I was a dramatist, he asked me a hundred questions about our theatres, and expressed a great desire to visit the States. All the actors were men, as the Japanese do not care to see women on the stage. The star and leading people had commodious dressing-rooms, their changes of costume were arranged on pegs upon the walls, and they were attended by dressers and barbers just like our own actors, the only difference being that they squatted on the floor while making their changes, and used metal mirrors instead of glass ones.

The *inari machi* (supers) dressed in a common room and were the apprentices of the various actors. There was nothing novel in the arrangements behind the scenes, everything being as inflammable and bare looking as in our own places of amusement. While we were chatting, the signal was given for the curtain to be drawn, hearing which we bade adieu to the actors and managers and returned to our boxes, where we remained until the entertainment concluded.

The second piece was of even a more sanguinary nature than the first, and I felt heartily glad to behold the last head severed and the gallant hero close his eyes in mimic death.

As we emerged upon the street the bell of a neighboring temple began to toll, and on consulting my watch I found that I had spent twelve hours in a Japanese theatre.

LEGENDS OF THE GOD-FOX.

IN a secluded part of the Kaga Yashiki, Tokio, stands a magnificent *sugi* (cedar), beneath the shadow of which is a dismantled shrine of Inari (the god of rice). Beside the ruin, half buried in the rank grass, lie two stone foxes, that formerly guarded the sacred spot, and, though once the object of profound veneration, now serve as "horses" for the children of the foreign professors who dwell within the walls of the *yashiki*. The red *torii* (archway) that spanned the approach was long ago converted into kindling by the *momban* (gate-keeper), the pathways are choked with weeds, and, save the before-mentioned little ones, few persons frequent the picturesque nook. Twenty-five years ago, when I first visited Yedo (Tokio), the Lord of Kaga and his ten thousand retainers lived in the *yashiki*, and the shrine and its guardians were kept in repair; now the noble is in retirement, the grounds contain a hospital and the residences of foreign teachers, and his brave retainers are scattered all over the empire, earning precarious livings by following peaceful occupations, starving, or pulling the *jin-riki-sha* of the hated *to-jin* (stranger)

One afternoon, while I was sitting beneath the tree, musing on the changes that had taken place in the Land of the Rising Sun, a Japanese, dressed in the garb of a pilgrim, approached, and noticing me, bowed and said, "A thousand pardons for thus intruding upon your honorable presence. I was once a retainer of the Lord of Kaga, and resided in this *yashiki*. I now live in my old province many *ri* from here."

Understanding that he had come upon a pilgrimage to the place, I arose to retire and leave him to his prayers, when he begged me to remain, saying, —

"I would like to ask a favor of you. My honorable mother, who is at the point of death, desires to have a stone from this shrine. Would you object to my removing a portion of it?"

I explained that I was only a visitor, and, therefore, had no power to grant his request, adding, —

"There is nobody looking. If the possession of a fragment of the ruin will benefit your honorable parent, why not help yourself?"

This appeared to please him greatly, and after praying fervently at the shrine, he removed a section of one of the moss-covered pillars, tied it in a square of blue cotton, lighted his pipe, and sitting upon his heels, said, —

"Inari is a very powerful god, and this spot was formerly the resort of many pilgrims and pious persons. I could tell you some wonderful stories concerning the god and his servants. You doubtless are curious to know why my honorable mother is so anxious to have a relic from this shrine. I will tell you. Though she had been married many years, and had prayed to the gods and continually made offerings, her petitions remained unanswered. One evening when she was passing this place, she thought she would supplicate the benevolent Inari." (In a low voice, regarding the overturned images.) "As she concluded her prayer, those god-foxes wagged their tails and the snow began to descend. Accepting the omens as favorable ones, she returned to her residence, on reaching which she was accosted by a miserable *yeta* [beggar], who, prostrating himself, cried piteously for something to eat. It so happened that the only food in the house was some red bean rice, which my mother had saved for her own consumption; however, her benevolence overcame every other feeling, and she generously presented the dish to the man, who immediately vanished taking the vessel with him. The next day, as my father was passing this shrine, he saw the platter lying on the ground before it, and on reaching home told my mother of the circumstance, whereupon she said, —

"'The *yeta* was the god-fox. Now I am a happy woman.'

"From that time she daily returned thanks to Inari and his servants. When I was old enough to understand, she brought me here and assisted me to make my first offering. All my life I have been under the protection of the god-fox."

He relighted his pipe, regarded me complacently and said,—

"I suppose you do no believe in such things? Well, everybody has his faith. You think one way and I another. Inari is a very powerful god and a very reliable one, and his servants are most kind and benevolent to those who worship him."

He spoke in a serious manner, and evidently believed what he said.

"Can you tell me something else about the god-fox?" I asked.

"I could give you a thousand proofs of his goodness to those who believe in Inari. Have you ever heard of the conversion of Raiko?"

"No," I answered.

"Ah!" (knocking the ashes from his pipe and regarding me with a compassionate air,) "you are to be pitied. Well, it is said that the gods will not condemn those who have never been taught the truth. I believe, after you have heard what I am about to relate, you will venerate Inari and his attendants."

He relighted his pipe, puffed at it for a few seconds, and continued: —

"Raiko was a very great man in his village. No one had such a long train of servants, such large ricefields, or extensive plantations; notwithstanding which, and though everything he undertook was a success, he was miserably stingy. He carried his money in his *obi* [girdle], and his meanness in his face; and no *yeta* [beggar] ever thought of soliciting him for a *rin* [mill], Raiko's visage being like a sign-board that warns trespassers from a field of grain Oh! he was a miserable fellow; still, because of his riches, the neighbors paid the man great respect and consulted him upon every important matter. As he grew older, he became more miserly and began to rack his brains how to save a few extra coins.

"One night, when he lay awake hugging his treasure, he counted the number of his servants on his fingers, then muttered, —

"'It is very foolish for a poor person like myself to support such a greedy, lazy crowd. I will dismiss them, and in future will attend to my own wants. What a wasteful fool I have been!'

"This thought so preyed upon his mind that he was

presently seized with a fever, which grew worse and worse, and threatened to burn up his very bones. His faithful servants watched him most tenderly, and did not heed his bad-tempered, reproachful utterances.

"'Ah!' he would exclaim, 'if I had been wiser, you would not have caused me to suffer this horrible sickness.'

"The fever lasted for several days, during which his spirits were low and his body became reduced to a shadow. On the tenth night, as he was rolling from side to side on his bed, a poorly dressed *bozu* suddenly appeared by his pillow, and, kneeling, regarded him sternly, then said, —

"'Hello, Raiko, how do you feel? Are you no better? I scarcely expected to find you here.'

"'Why not?' growled the sufferer.

"'I thought the *oni* [imps] would have carried you off by this time,' coolly responded the *bozu*.

"'Who are you, who come thus unannounced into my bedchamber?' angrily demanded the sick man. 'As for the imps, they are no worse than you, *bozu*. I have never troubled you or entered your temples; so now, I beg you will walk out of my house. I know what you have come after. You always wait until people are sick, then threaten them with the torments of hell. You need not imagine you will ever see the glitter of my money.'

"The *bozu*, instead of being angry, laughed heartily, and replied, —

"'Listen, Raiko, I do not covet any of your ill-gotten gains. We *bozu* are very particular whose money we handle. We live to perform good deeds, not to accumulate wealth. Do you wish to be cured of your sickness? Oh, you need not turn your back upon me! I know a sovereign remedy for your disease.'

"'I suppose, if you cure me, you will want to be paid for it,' snarled Raiko.

"'Not a *rin*, not a *rin*,' laughingly answered the *bozu*. 'You are so mean that you imagine every one is the same. Shall I tell you the cure, or leave you to die?'

"Raiko half rose in bed, and, surlily regarding the *bozu*, grumbled, —

"'If you promise not to ask any recompense, I will hear your remedy.'

"'It is this,' said the visitor. 'Loosen your *obi* [girdle], you miserable, selfish man, and let your wealth fall for those who need it. If you still keep it bound about you, it will cause your death.'

"'*Yeh!*' furiously exclaimed Raiko, snatching a dagger from his bosom. 'Though you are a priest, I will kill you! I will never part with my hard-earned money.'

"The *bozu* uttered a derisive laugh, and retreating a few paces, said, —

"'Wretch! I will now tell you the truth. I overheard your mean resolve to dismiss your faithful servants, and have nightly visited you, and drained a portion of your life-blood. Now I will finish you, and strangers shall enjoy your carefully hoarded gold.'

"As he uttered these words, he blew out the light, and Raiko felt some dreadful object advance and attack him. The miser, thinking only of his money, vigorously defended himself, and as he did so, uttered loud cries that attracted the attention of his servants, who crowded into the room and anxiously inquired the cause of his alarm.

"'Bring me a light, quickly!' he cried. 'I have wounded that *bozu*, who, I believe, was a robber in disguise.'

"When lanterns were brought Raiko beheld the hairy, horny claw of a monster lying by the side of his mat, seeing which he said, —

"'Whatever that is, follow and kill it. You ought to be ashamed of yourselves for leaving me here alone. I have nearly met my death.'

"The faithful men bowed respectfully, and tracing his assailant by the tiny drops of blood on the mats, followed it into the furthermost part of the garden, where, scooped out of a little artificial *yama* [mountain], they discovered a large hole, from whence protruded the head and shoulders of an enormous spider, who thus addressed them: —

"'Do not seek to attack the gods, but retire and persuade your master to atone for his sin of covetousness, which has almost destroyed him.'

"The trembling listeners prostrated themselves and promised obedience, then returned to the house and delivered the message to Raiko. The latter heard them respectfully, and felt remorse for his conduct. He repented and gave large sums of money to the *bozu* and poor, and lived to a good old age."

Then the speaker stopped, regarded me significantly, and murmured, —

"Now, what do you think of the god-fox?"

"I do not quite see what he had to do with it," I responded.

The man looked at the overturned stone figures, and once more lowering his voice, continued, —

"Don't you understand? The spider was one of the many shapes assumed by the god-fox."

Finding that he was in a humor to continue his stories, I begged he would relate something more concerning his favorite deity; hearing which he smiled, bowed, and said, —

"There was another covetous man who lived in the

same town as Raiko. This fellow was a carpenter, who used to say, —

"'If I only had a second pair of hands, how much I would accomplish and how rich I would grow!'

"One night he prayed to the gods to give him a second pair of hands, and on awakening in the morning discovered that his petition had been granted. Delighted with the benevolence of the deities, he went to work with a will and performed the labor of two people. After a while his meanness overcame his delight, and he thought, —

"'If I only had six hands, how much more work I could do. Oh! for six hands.'

"Again the grasping wretch petitioned, and once more his request was granted; but, by and by, he once more began to sigh and moan, and finally he asked the gods to give him eight hands, promising he would be satisfied with that number. To his delight the additional blessings were vouchsafed him, and for a while he was really contented. One day a travelling showman appeared before the carpenter's shop, and after regarding him attentively, said, —

"'What a foolish fellow you are to work as you do! If you will come with me I will exhibit you, and will make your fortune while you are winking. I know millions of people who would give all they possess to behold such a curiosity as you are.'

"He talked so pleasantly and used such skilful arguments, that the covetous dupe yielded and crawled into the cage provided by his tempter. As soon as the foolish fellow had entered the trap, the showman locked him in and conveyed his prize from village to village. Instead of reaping a golden harvest, the many-handed man was half starved and was exhibited for a few *rin* to every person who wished to gape at him. When he expostulated, his master prodded him with a pointed stick and made him feel sore all over, in addition to which his tormentor told people that his victim was an Aino from Yezo."

The pilgrim then paused, elevated his eyebrows, regarded me slyly, and murmured, —

"Of course you understand that the showman was Inari's servant."

"Why do you permit your gods to lie there in such a disgraceful position?" I inquired. "If I were you I would place them upright."

This suggestion appeared to please him greatly, and he advanced, set the stone foxes upon their bases, bowed to each, picked up the cloth containing the relic from the shrine, gravely saluted and retired, leaving me listening to the shrill notes of the *semi* (tree locust) chirping in the boughs of the old *sugi*, and pondering over the legends of the god-fox.

NO GAKU.
(ANCIENT OPERA OF JAPAN.)

DURING my last visit to Tokio, I was invited to witness a *no* performance, given by the members of the Maple Club, an association of Japanese gentlemen who own a beautiful place at Royokwan in Shiba.

The *no gaku* is of very ancient origin, and is a combination of slow pantomime, dancing, and high-flown, long-drawn sentences, intoned in a language as unintelligible to the ordinary Japanese as Italian is to the mass of our people.

As a relic of the primitive forms of opera and drama, it is highly interesting, but were it not for the comparatively modern farces called *no-kio-gen*, that are introduced between the *no gaku*, the entertainment would be exceedingly wearisome to the foreigner.

One charming afternoon in May I accompanied some American friends to Royokwan, where we were received and welcomed by the officials of the club. After visiting the handsomely decorated rooms of the main building, we were conducted to the theatre, — a neatly built, shed-like structure of white-wood, which was filled with Japanese of the better class, who like ourselves were guests of the members. A gentlemanly committee-man, dressed in full American evening costume, minus the shoes, — which are never worn indoors, — showed us to our chairs in the front row, and presented each of our party with a lithographed programme in English.

The native portion of the audience squatted on the matted floor of the centre and left wing of the building, while the ladies and children were accommodated in a separate shed on our right. Before us was a roofed platform of white-wood, enclosed with railings of the same material, the back being furnished with a screen on which was painted a gnarled *matsu* (pine-tree). This and an oblong, lacquered tablet, inscribed with the characters *No Gaku* (*no* opera), and decorated with two massive scarlet silk tassels, was the only ornamentation of the stage, the entire arrangement being exquisitely simple and restful to the eyes.

Upon our left was the actors' dressing-room, which was connected with the stage by a bridge of unpainted white-wood, furnished with a simple railing of the same material.

About four o'clock the curtain veiling the entrance to the dressing-room was raised by elevating its corners on poles, and five musicians entered silently, crossed the bridge, crouched at the back of the stage, prostrated themselves and performed the respectful salutation, after which, sitting upon their heels, they remained as motionless as statues.

In a few moments the chorus, consisting of ten amateurs clothed in gray silk robes, and wearing the *kamishimo* (wing-shaped upper garment), entered, and moving like spirits over the bridge, knelt in two rows on the left of the stage, then saluted in the same manner as the musicians had done.

"Now," said a Japanese friend on my left, producing a pocket edition of the plays, which he politely proffered to me, "prepare to be delighted. All the characters will be represented by celebrated *no* performers."

The entertainment commenced by the flute player executing some weird *staccato* passages, then a lean singer on his left contorted his visage and proceeded to indulge in most agonizing howls. He whooped, imitated a person suffering from pangs of seasickness, and strained himself in a manner painful to behold, his efforts being vigorously seconded by his next neighbor, a fat little fellow with a head as bald as a polished cocoanut.

Although their exertions nearly caused the foreign portion of the audience to choke with suppressed laughter, the Japanese spectators evidently enjoyed the demoniacal sounds, for they listened with grave and interested countenances, just as lovers of Italian singing do to a *tour de force* of one of our operatic stars.

At the conclusion of the infernal sounds, the *Tsudzumi uchi* (player on a small drum, shaped like an hour-glass), and an operator on a little sieve-shaped drum, beaten with two long sticks, who had been eagerly watching the soloists, as though waiting for their cue, struck their instruments vigorously, and shrieked approvingly, " *Yee-haa!* "

When they had repeated this thrice, the chorus began a low, musical Gregorian-like chant that, after the barbarous noises to which we had been treated, sounded like a heavenly song.

While they were intoning, the curtain of the dressing-room was raised, and a stern-looking man, costumed in the garb of a priest, wearing a *zu-kin* (white head-dress, shaped like a mob-cap), and having the lower portion of his face covered with a towel, slowly advanced upon the bridge, and halting, regarded us "with glittering eyes." His garments were drawn up about his waist, exhibiting his bare limbs and white *tabi* (socks), and over his left shoulder he carried a *naga-nata* (long spear), the staff of which was beautifully decorated and lacquered.

"That is Musashibo-benkei," whispered my friend. "Now you will hear something good. The gentleman who takes that part is one of our most talented *no* performers."

The actor advanced slowly, like a school-boy summoned to receive chastisement, and upon reaching the front of the stage executed a stately dance, then chanted in a deeply tragic voice, "I am Musashibo-benkei, the priest of Saito Kitadani. In fulfilment of a vow I have been in the Ginsenji for seven days, and to-night I go to Kitano on my way to Ushinotoki-mari." (Calls his servant.)

Chorus, responding for the latter: "I think you had better not go to-night."

Benkei, in a guttural, dramatic voice: "Why so?"

Chorus: "Last night, when we were passing the Tojo bridge, a young fellow, twelve or thirteen years old, attacked us with a small sword. He was as quick as a butterfly in his movements, and threatened to kill us; so beware of him."

Benkei, in a contemptuous voice, singing out of the left corner of his mouth: "Though he were as quick as a butterfly, you should have surrounded him and cut him down."

Chorus: "When we surrounded him he sprang over our heads, and our blows fell upon each other."

Benkei (derisively): "If you had attacked him actively you must have slain him."

Chorus: "He is a supernatural being. Indeed, no one could kill him. Though this is a great city, it has no other such extraordinary being as he in it."

Benkei (thoughtfully aside): "Then I think I will not start for Ushinotoki-mari to-night."

Chorus: "That will be excellent."

Benkei (slowly and bombastically): "It shall never be said that Musashibo-benkei was frightened by stories of brigands. To-night I will take my stand, alone, upon the bridge and conquer that extraordinary person."

Then he slowly raised his spear and with it performed a number of wonderful evolutions, sometimes remaining several minutes in one pose, during which the chorus intoned a long description of the hero Ushiwaka (a name of Yoshitsuni), and ended with the following: —

"At the hour of midnight, the bell of Santo rang out clear upon the air. All was still and the moon shone brightly. When the sound of the bell had ceased, Benkei advanced upon the bridge. He was dressed in his loose armor of black leather, and carried over his shoulder his favorite *naga-nata*. His appearance would have frightened demons, and he was well satisfied with himself."

Benkei (in a deep, tragic tone): "I am Musashibo-benkei. I fear no one."

Chorus: "Benkei slowly paced the bridge and trod heavily upon the planks."

Benkei (in a hoarse, deep voice): "I am Musashibo-benkei. Who dares to cross weapons with me?"

He stamped alternately with his right and left foot, scowled ferociously and moved majestically up the stage, while the flute player began a weird air and his eccentric companions again imitated persons suffering from *mal-de-mer*. During this excruciating performance, the curtain of the dressing-room was once more raised, and a youth clad in silken upper garments and immensely wide *hakama* (trousers) of white silk, the size of which was made more conspicuous by the insertion of a broad stiffening, glided across the bridge and descending the stage, began to deliver a speech in a high-pitched monotone.

He was a chubby-faced, brown-skinned, good-looking young gentleman, and was fully impressed with a sense of his own ability. His coarse, black hair, worn in the modern foreign style, was bound with a white fillet, the long ends of which floated down his back, and in his *obi* (girdle) he carried a short and a long sword.

After indulging in a prolonged speech, he turned suddenly and revealed the expansive back of his lower garment. This action, though intended to be highly dramatic, excited the risibility of the foreign portion of the audience, heedless of which he strutted, stamped, and gestured defiantly, while the chorus intoned, "Ushiwaka rejoiced to see Benkei, and covering his face with a thin cloth, stood still."

The young actor veiled his features, and slowly advanced up the stage; while at the same time Benkei descended it, eying him askance and chanting in a significant tone, "I am a priest, therefore I will not look at her."

As he passed Ushiwaka, the latter extended his foot sideways, and kicked the end of the old man's *naganata* (spear), whereupon the warrior scowled and chanted in thundering tones, "Impolite creature, I will frighten you!"

He raised his weapon and made a pass with it, seeing which Ushiwaka turned, threw aside his veil, and drawing his sword, stood on the defensive. Then followed an ideal combat; the Japanese, in their stage battles, mimicking instead of delivering blows.

Chorus: "Benkei was the inferior in the art of war and was gradually driven back."

Benkei (pausing and regarding Ushiwaka from under his bushy eyebrows): "There is no reason why I should be beaten by such a youth as this."

Chorus (during which the two actors slowly illustrated the recitative): "Benkei cut transversely at Ushiwaka, but the latter jumped aside. Then he slashed at the young man's legs, when Ushiwaka sprang into the air. As Benkei delivered a blow at his opponent's head or neck, the youth crouched upon the ground. At last Ushiwaka, tired of acting on the defensive, attacked Benkei, and wounding his hand, caused him to drop his spear. Finding himself disarmed, the old man tried to close with his assailant; but so skilfully did Ushiwaka use his sword that he was unable to get near him."

Benkei (in a tremulous, enraged tone): "I know not what to do! Tell me your name."

Ushiwaka: "I will confess the truth." (Proudly.) "I am Minamoto no Ushiwaka."

Benkei (falling upon his knees): "The son of Yoshitomo!" (Bowing his head to the ground and yielding.)

Ushiwaka (grandly surveying him): "Who are you?"

Benkei (respectfully sucking in his breath, and replying with his head close to the boards, in a low monotone): "I am Saito no Musashibo-benkei."

Chorus (bowing low and singing in a loud, triumphant manner): "Benkei begged pardon for his rudeness, and went to Kujo with Ushiwaka."

At the conclusion of this song, the younger actor slowly strutted off the stage and across the bridge, followed at a respectful distance by the conquered Benkei. As the actors disappeared behind the curtain, the musicians once more indulged in their wild strains and the solo singers again treated us to their soul-moving performances, after which they and the chorus rose and departed noiselessly.

The next piece was a *no-kio-gen* (farce) called "Ishigami."

A woman who has a drunken husband and desires to be separated from him consults the *nakato* (middle-man) who had brought about their marriage. The go-between, who is a waggish fellow, tells her to relate her troubles to the god Ishigami; then seeking the husband, gives him the mask and robe of the deity, and instructs him what to do. The wife goes to a thanksgiving festival in honor of Ishigami, and approaching the figure, which is her husband in disguise, kneels, and after bowing respectfully, pours out her sorrows, recounting such a list of complaints that the husband pushes the mask on to the top of his head and regards her with comical amazement, saying in a sly aside, "I did not know that I was half as bad as she makes out."

"Yes, yes, he is a thoroughly mean fellow," cries the woman, with her head still bowed. "He is a lazy, shiftless, good-for-nothing *norakura-mono* [vagabond], and I have had about enough of him."

This speech caused the mock god to grind his teeth and to replace his mask with a quick gesture, as though desirous of shutting out her voice. After treating him to much plain talk, she assumed an upright position, gazed tearfully and pleadingly at the goggle-eyed visor, and folding her hands palm to palm, continued, "Great Ishigami, what do you advise me to do?"

"Woman," he replied in a hollow voice, "while loading your husband with ten thousand crimes, you forget it is your conduct that has driven him to seek consolation in the *saké* cup. Your tongue sounds like a bird rattle agitated by the breeze. You ought to have drowned yourself instead of coming here and so shamelessly denouncing your lord and master."

On hearing these harsh words she again bowed her head, and tearfully replied, —

"I know I am very weak; still it is hard to bear with a man who drinks like a *shojo* [river demigod who is fond of *saké*]. I admit that I have allowed my tongue to run somewhat freely. Pardon me, merciful Ishigami."

While she was speaking, he once more pushed up his mask, and placing his arms akimbo, chuckled triumphantly to himself. In the midst of his merriment she suddenly raised her head to apply her sleeves to her eyes, whereupon he once more jerked down the mask, refolded his hands, and assumed a godlike pose, saying, —

"Some people are never satisfied. Woman, what do you want? Have you not a handsome young husband, who is the admiration of all your friends and neighbors? You ought to be united to some poor, miserable, surly-tempered, withered old fellow, who would make you slave from morn till night, and never give you a holiday. No wonder you weep with shame."

This caused her to sob worse than before, and to bury her face in the sleeves of her *kimono*. During the progress of her lamentations he turned adroitly on his seat, and shifting his mask to the back of his head, waited for her reply.

Presently she raised her tear-moistened face to the visor, and not perceiving the change in his position, said, —

"Powerful Ishigami, do not overwhelm me with your wrath. You know not how bad it is to have a drunken brute come home at night and break things. I have borne this until my bosom is wellnigh closed with grief. Look kindly on me and relieve me from my misery."

Then, hysterically raising her voice, she once more

recounted her husband's imperfections; upon hearing which he silently rose, placed his fingers in his ears, and retreated up the stage. For several moments she continued to address the block on which he had been seated, while he stood at the upper part of the stage, and expressed his delight in the most comical pantomime. At length she discovered his absence, and after gaping some time at the empty seat, rose and gazed about her with a terrified countenance, whereupon he quickly turned and presented his back to her. She moved after him, bowing at every step, and drying her eyes on her sleeves, shrieked her complaints as volubly as before; but whenever she neared him he nimbly retreated. Sometimes he crouched, and slipping the visor on to the top of his head, presented it toward her and pretended to listen; then he would adroitly turn and place the mask over one of his ears, as he did so grimacing derisively.

After a long chase, he resumed his seat and said, " I never had such a persistent suppliant. If you worry your husband as much as you have done me, I am not surprised at his indulging in an extra cup of *saké*. You ought to make a vow to abstain from talking during the remainder of your life."

This advice appeared greatly to affect the woman, who, throwing herself at his feet, once more began to weep bitterly. While she was lamenting, he removed the mask from his face, calmly fanned himself with it, regarded her triumphantly, and finally, becoming careless, uttered a snicker of satisfaction. Before he could replace his visor, she raised her head and discovered the cheat that had been put upon her; whereupon she scolded furiously and drove him round and round the stage, he alternately laughing and pretending to be very penitent. When she had thoroughly exhausted her anger, he coaxed her back into a good-humor; then, making a significant grimace, said, —

"Now we will go home and live peaceably. After unburdening your soul, you will feel more comfortable. I here solemnly vow to Ishigami never again to drink more than one cup of *saké* at a time"; adding in a sly aside, "I have only one mouth, and an empty cup can always be refilled."

The by-play of the performers was excellent, and their points were made quietly, without glancing significantly at the audience. During the farce the orchestra and chorus were absent from the stage, but on its conclusion they returned silently.

The next piece was called *Momijigari* (hunting among the maples): a very old play, in which Taira Korimochi, a general of the eleventh century, meets an *oni* (ghoul) disguised as a beautiful woman, and is drawn into conversation with her. Warned of her true nature by the god Hachiman (chorus), he kills her and escapes. The costume of Kórimochi and the masks and dresses of the spirit and her attendants were most elaborate and gorgeous; but their tedious speeches proved almost too much for the foreign portion of the audience, and we were glad when the *Momijigari* was concluded, and the stage cleared for a farce called *Hanaori* (the flower plucking), the plot of which was as follows:—

An old *bozu*, going on a journey, charges his assistant not to admit any one to see the cherry blossoms in the temple grounds. No sooner has the aged man departed than a crowd (represented by five people) clamors at the gate and asks to be permitted to see the flowers. Finally, the young *bozu* good-humoredly admits them, and partakes of *saké* until he becomes intoxicated and tumbles on to the boards; when the people rob the cherry-trees (represented by a branch placed in a wooden frame) and retire, chanting a bacchanalian song. All the action of the piece was in pantomime; the performers pretended to drink *saké* from their fans and to admire imaginary *sakura* (cherry) trees, represented by the artificial branch.

The most amusing portion was when the old priest returned and discovered his disciple prone on the ground. He approached him with an expression of the greatest amazement, and, bending, sniffed suspiciously; then, applying his thumb and forefinger to his nostrils, muttered the single word "*saké*" (rice wine), and made an exit worthy of a first-class comedian.

The last play, while apparently interesting to the Japanese, was wearisome to the foreign guests, some of the speeches occupying twenty minutes in their delivery. The principal performers were a red-headed *shojo*, who moved like an automaton, and Kofu, a *saké* seller. They strutted, howled, mouthed, and ranted, very much after the fashion of our old-time actors, and appeared as though they intended to talk all night. The sun was setting when the demon made his exit, and the chorus, after reciting a short epilogue, wound up to the accompaniment of the flute and drum and the unearthly whooping of the soloists.

I believe, though the young nobles of Nihon profess to admire the mechanical acting and the inflated delivery affected by the performers, they infinitely prefer the elaborate feast, good wine, graceful dancing, and lively modern songs of the *geisha* that usually follow the *no gaku*.

SHINDA USAGI-UMA.

(LEGEND OF THE DEAD ASS.)

AMONG the many tales exposing the craft of the Buddhist priests, none is more witty and effective than that of the *Shinda Usagi-uma,* which is said to be over fifteen hundred years old. It is often recited by Japanese story-tellers, but it has never before, to my knowledge, been told in English.

The *hanashika* who related the following was a wrinkled, sly-looking fellow, who perfectly understood his profession, and could at will excite his audience to laughter, tears, or outbursts of indignation.

Having sent round his fan for the preliminary collection, he bowed respectfully, and commenced in a quiet, somewhat monotonous voice, —

"The ancient philosophers asserted that there was a *shinda usagi-uma* [dead ass] in every faith. This I will prove to you by the story of the Chinese priest; therefore listen, honorable sirs, and let me illuminate your souls.

"Many years ago a pious *bozu* dwelt in a little temple

in the province of Honan. He was considered to be almost a saint, so perfect was his life, so calm, so ascetic the appearance of his face." (In a comical tone.) "Oh, it is so easy to be serene of countenance when there are plenty of credulous people to find you in rice and wine!"

"*Hai!*" (an ejaculation like "yes!") from the audience. "*Hai! hai! hai!*"

The *hanashika* sipped a mouthful of water, bowed, and continued in his ordinary voice, —

"Yes, he was a pious man. He rose before daybreak, prayed continually, listened patiently to the foolish stories of the girls and old women who crowded to his retreat, and chuckled inwardly when he heard the coins fall into the money-box. He was a perfect example of his class; his life being passed in" (satirically) " doing nothing.

"In the rear of the little altar of the temple was a tomb, carefully protected by a wooden grating, through which the faithful thrust their hands to touch the slab covering the bones of the saint, and thus rid themselves of the hundred million curses of humanity. Wonderful is the power of a dead saint." (Slyly.) "Wait until I die, honorable sirs: my bones will cure your diseases better than any patent medicine."

"*Hai!*" (Laughingly, by the audience.) "*Yuke!* [Go on!]"

The *hanashika* closed his twinkling eyes and said, —
"The *bozu*, like all his brotherhood, had an assistant; he also kept a white ass to carry his disciple when the latter visited the faithful who resided afar. You know that it is impossible for a holy being, who is praying continually, to use his limbs like a *jin-riki-sha* man. In our cities the bald-heads [derisive term for a Buddhist priest] are carried in litters; but in China they ride on asses, — a sign of humility, for as everybody knows, the *bozu* are very meek and humble.

"As the years passed, the fame of the shrine and its guardian increased. Indeed, it was whispered abroad that the miraculous power of the sacred relics had become communicated to the person of the *bozu*, and that many pious believers had been relieved of their infirmities by simply gazing on the old man's face or touching the hem of his robe." (Chuckling.) "For my part, I prefer to seek the advice of a physician. The touch-cure never did me any good.

"The faithful brought wine, roasted ducks and pigs, and sweetmeats for the gods, and the altar was laden with offerings. When the *bozu* and his disciple ate their frugal meal of rice, and drank water from the spring, the deities smiled approvingly. It was wonderful how much *saké* the images drank, and how eagerly they gobbled up the offerings, never so much as leaving a grease mark or the odor of wine in the vessels to gratify the noses of their attendants." (Slyly.) "But then, *bozu* do not thirst after intoxicating drink, or desire to eat forbidden food like us sinners; no, indeed! they are holy beings who have burnt *moxa* on their heads, and vowed to abstain from all nice things. Oh! honorable sirs, who would be a *bozu*, to exist on rice, never so much as sniff at a winecup or look admiringly on a pretty flower? You remember the proverb, 'Those who serve the gods must be contented with the fragrance of the offerings.' The happiness arising from a holy life makes the *bozu* sleek."

The audience roared their approval of his sarcasm, and showered the brass *cash* upon the mat before him. Then he bowed gravely and resumed his story: —

"The *bozu* grew fat through sanctity, and his disciple waxed lusty from the same cause, when, alas! a famine swept over the province. Pious persons were no longer able to bring offerings to the gods; and the younger *bozu*, not being endowed with miraculous power, became as thin as a crane's leg, and as weak as thrice-diluted *saké*, while the old one remained as plump as a well-fed mouse.

"One morning, when they were mechanically repeating their prayers, a sudden faintness overpowered the disciple, who, forgetting his vows, exclaimed abruptly,

'Look here, I have had about enough of this! How do you contrive to keep fat without eating?'

"For some minutes his superior was too much amazed to reply. However, he presently resumed his usual ascetic manner and said, 'My son, you must have more faith. Thrice a day I touch the bones of the sainted one resting under the slab at the back of the altar, and am sustained. *Namu Amida Butsu!* [Hail, Omnipotent Buddha!]'

"The lad pondered over this speech, and resolved to test the efficacy of the relics. That afternoon, when his superior was listening to the pitiful stories of some starving women, he crept to the sacred spot, and prostrating himself, inserted his hands between the bars, when, to his astonishment, he touched a —"

Here the *hanashika* paused, and bowing, said, "Honorable sirs, if you will give me a few *tempo*, I will continue my story; but if your purses are exhausted, I can wait until another day."

"Go on!' yelled his delighted audience, liberally responding to his request, — "go on! go on! go on!"

He sipped a cup of tea, gathered up the contributions, and when he had slipped the last coin into his sleeve, said in a sly, satirical voice, —

"The disciple touched a gourd like those used by pilgrims. 'Benevolent gods!' he murmured, 'this must be a relic of the immortal saint. Probably its miraculous contents have enabled my superior to retain his strength and look so nice and fat. What is good for the dog is excellent for the puppy.'

"Shaking the vessel and applying his snub nose to the stopper, he continued, 'There can be no harm in my tasting this holy water.'

"He reverently removed the wooden plug from the neck of the vessel, raised the latter to his parched lips, closed his eyes, and — was sustained! That night, when he thought his superior was slumbering, he rose from his mat and returned to the tomb. He was about to resume his devotions, when he discovered the *bozu* seated on the grating with the empty gourd in his hand.

"'My son,' said the aged man, in a voice husky with emotion, 'the revenue of the temple will no longer — hic — sustain two of us; the thistles are daily becoming scarcer, and our faithful — hic — animal will soon be as — hic — thin as we are. You must take him and go to a country where there is no famine. Leave me here to die at my — hic — post!'

"Then, weak with fasting and prayer, he sank upon the tomb and slumbered like an infant on its mother's bosom.

"At daybreak the disciple rose and was about to set

out on his journey, when he heard the voice of the *bozu* calling feebly, 'Come back! come back! I must give you my blessing, or you will never prosper.'

"The lad returned and knelt while the old man blessed him, thinking, 'Every moment I remain here increases my hunger. I want to depart and to seek a new retreat, where I can practise our holy faith in its purity. How prone men are to deceit!'

"Though he thought this, he murmured in response to his superior's blessing, '*Namu Amida Butsu!*'

"After saying farewell he mounted the ass, and turning his back upon the little temple, started upon his journey into the unknown country, sighing at the duplicity of his master and feeling certain that the gods would punish the old man for his impiety.

"'Ah!' he sighed. 'Would that I were able to carry off the sacred relics and enshrine them in a spot where I could sit and meditate from dawn till eve! I fear, spite of his reputation, my venerated teacher is at heart a hypocrite, and that he, not the gods, drank the wine brought by the faithful.'

"Meditating thus, he rode on and on, until he reached a country where there was no famine, where the men walked with their stomachs projecting, the women were pious and kind to holy persons, and his steed revelled in the sweet grass growing on the roadside.

"One day, when the sun was high in the heavens, the animal, heretofore so sturdy and vigorous, suddenly began to tremble, and presently, dropping upon its knees, 'uttered its last prayer' and died. This unexpected calamity rendered the young *bozu* almost speechless with grief. All he could do was to kneel beside the motionless form, clasp his hands palm to palm, and ejaculate, '*Namu Amida Butsu! Namu Amida Butsu!*'

"While he was thus employed, a man wearing the peculiar collar denoting that he was favored of the gods [insane or idiotic] approached him, and after listening awhile, derisively exclaimed, —

"'How remarkable! A *bozu* earnestly and reverently calling on Buddha! A quack swallowing his own medicine! Here, take my collar and give me your *kesa* [sacred scarf]. If you do not know what to do with your dead brother, I will tell you. You should be the fool and I the *bozu*.'

"'I fail to comprehend your words,' said the agitated one. 'What can I do if Buddha does not restore this poor creature to life?'

"The fool approached close to the mourner and slyly whispered, 'Make a good living out of its carcass.'

"'I do not understand you.'

"'No! Ha, ha! Which of us is the fool?'

"'How can I make a livelihood out of a dead animal?' demanded the mourner. 'If this were a holy person, I might,—but an ass—' (Sighing.) '*Namu Amida Butsu! Namu Amida Butsu!*'

"The fool uttered a cry of derision, then said, 'We certainly ought to change places. Listen to me! I will teach you your business. Cover that body with earth, kneel at a respectful distance from it, address Buddha in your usual senseless manner, and between your prayers say to the passers-by, "If you would spare yourselves torment in a future state, contribute a few coins toward building a temple over this sinless one!"'

"The *bozu* gaped with amazement, then demanded, 'Well, what good will that do?'

"'You dull-head,' angrily returned the fool, 'where have you been trained? Do you not understand there are plenty of credulous, ignorant believers in Buddha, who, imagining that to be the body of a saint, will give you any amount of money? Thousand gods! I wish I had your chance. I shall burst my liver laughing at your stupidity!'

"He then made a gesture of contempt and walked on.

"When the simple one was out of sight, the *bozu* carefully covered the animal with earth, and kneeling at a few paces from the mound, placed his bowl before him, and alternately prayed to Buddha and cried to the spectators, 'If you would spare yourselves torment in a future state, contribute a few *tempo* toward raising a tomb over this sinless one.'

"When the shadows of evening fell, the bowl was heaped with money, and that night the *bozu* ate and drank like any sinner. The next morning he resumed his place by the body, and excited the fears and charity of the wayfarers by his whining petitions. Toward evening, as the sun was casting long shadows, he saw a poor carpenter slowly returning from a hard day's toil.

"'My son,' he said, 'if you would save yourself from a thousand years of torment, build a fence round the remains of this sinless one.'

"In vain the unfortunate man pleaded that he was almost worn out. 'The pains of a thousand years in hell avoided by a few hours' work to-night,' said the *bozu*.

"Ere the bell in the neighboring temple struck the hour of the rat [midnight], the dupe had enclosed the remains with a neat railing and had gone home to die of exhaustion.

"Within a month from that time, bricks had taken the place of wood, and the *bozu* had built himself a handsome residence near the spot. Later on, a small temple was erected over the remains, the shrine was decorated with gilding and lacquer, and it soon became a famous place of pilgrimage; for, strange to say, the bones of the 'sinless one' worked miracles, often causing the deaf to hear, the blind to see, the lame to walk, and the dumb to speak.

"All this was not accomplished in a day; meanwhile the *bozu* grew as fat as *dai-koku-jin*, and when he walked looked not upon the ground, and when he ate and drank partook of more invigorating sustenance than rice and water. Around him gathered pious persons of both sexes, and it was said that no one could resist his saintly smile.

"One day, when he was meditating upon the hollowness of the world and upon the joys of celibacy, he remembered his aged superior, the *bozu* of Honan, and determined to pay him a visit, thinking, 'I will show him the folly of the sage's teaching, "Admirable is the wisdom of age, absurd the stupidity of youth." I once thought him deceitful because he kept his wine gourd in the saint's resting-place. Ah! he was a poor, simple-minded old man, and was only guilty of one sin, while I have committed many, and deceived millions of pious people. It will be an act of reparation to visit him and to take the good father some fine *saké*.'

"In a few days he set out on his pilgrimage, accompanied by a multitude of religious persons, who, while paying the expenses of his trip, were deluded into the belief that they were getting rid of a load of sin. The glorious orb of light was sinking behind the vermilion curtain when the cortége arrived at the little temple where the *bozu* had spent the peaceful hours of his novitiate. In the porch stood the attenuated superior, shading his blinking eyes with his withered shaking hands.

"'Ah!' murmured the old man, as the cavalcade drew near and the fat *bozu* dismounted. 'What have we here? A bishop conveying a company of pious nuns upon a pilgrimage? *Namu Amida Butsu!*'

"As he spoke the stranger approached, and kneeling, said, 'Holy Father! I am your humble disciple. Have you forgotten my insignificant existence?'

"He merely uttered these words for the sake of effect, he feeling a contempt for one who, for so many years, had been contented to remain in such a wretched place. Then he rose, ordered his servants to carry some gold-lacquered cases into the sanctuary, and said to his companions, 'Retire to the neighboring tea-houses until I join you. I desire to be alone with this venerable father.'

"The latter led the way to the sacred spot, and when the servants had left them, seated himself near the tomb, and inviting his visitor to follow his example, said, 'My son, Buddha has indeed blessed you.'

"The fat *bozu* withdrew a flask of *hana-zakari* [the flower in full bloom] from a case, extricated the plug from its neck with his teeth, poured out two cups of the generous liquid, and proffered one of them to his superior; after which he seated himself and related his adventures. In his haste he omitted to tell about meeting with the fool, and took all the credit of the idea to himself. During the progress of the recital, his host listened with half-closed eyes, and repeatedly exclaimed, 'Admirable is the wisdom of youth, absurd the stupidity of age'; then extended his cup to be refilled, and smiled benevolently.

"The visitor, flattered by his words, grew bold and ridiculed his former teacher, saying, 'After all, the sages were very ignorant men. It requires the keenness of youth to invent anything. While you have been eking out a miserable existence upon the relics of a genuine saint, I have lived in splendor on those of an ass. Confess, O holy father, that your disciple has been able to teach you something!'

"The ascetic glanced keenly at him, and gravely replied, 'My son, I do not envy you your grand temple, your dazzling shrine, your eloquent tongue, your success in making converts, your overflowing money chest, or your beautiful disciples: you are welcome to the fruits of your labor'; (once more extending his cup,)

'I no longer care for anything but attaining perfection. However, be not too greatly exalted by your own cleverness; and above all, do not imagine you know so much more than I do. What you deem to be a new idea is as old as the hills, and exists in some shape in all faiths and in all countries.'

"Then, lowering his voice to a whisper, he pointed his lean forefinger toward the tomb, and smiling until he exhibited the roots of his two fang-like teeth, added, 'My son, the mother of your ass lies buried there!'"

20 EAST SEVENTEENTH STREET,
Between Union Square and Fifth Avenue.

MY collection of Ancient and Modern Oriental Porcelain, Japanese Lacquers, Bronzes, Ivory Carvings, Kakémono, Screens, Curios, and Decorative Fabrics is open to the public from 10 A. M. to 5 P. M.

EDWARD GREEY.

www.ingramcontent.com/pod-product-compliance
Lightning Source LLC
Chambersburg PA
CBHW011342090426
42743CB00018B/3417